The Student-Centered Classroom Handbook

A Guide to Implementation

Volume One: Secondary Social Studies/History

Bil Johnson

EYE ON EDUCATION
6 DEPOT WAY WEST, SUITE 106
LARCHMONT, NY 10538
(914) 833–0551
(914) 833–0761 fax
www.eyeoneducation.com

Library of Congress Cataloging-in-Publication Data

Johnson, Bil, 1949-
   The student-centered classroom handbook : a guide to implementation / Bil Johnson.
      p. cm.
   Includes bibliographical references.
   Contents: v. 1. Secondary social studies/history
   ISBN 1-930556-49-7 (v. 1)
   1. Middle school teaching--Handbooks, manuals, etc. 2. High school teaching--Handbooks, manuals, etc. I. Title.

LB1607 .J59 2003
373.1102--dc21

                                                        2002029748

10 9 8 7 6 5 4 3 2 1

Editorial and production services provided by
Richard H. Adin Freelance Editorial Services
52 Oakwood Blvd., Poughkeepsie, NY 12603-4112
(845-471-3566)

DEDICATION

This book is dedicated to all the students I
have worked with over the last 30 years.

Meet the Author

Bil Johnson, a former public school social studies and English teacher, is currently Clinical Professor in Brown University's Education Department. The author of the highly successful **Performance Assessment Handbook** series, he won the William McLaughlin Award for Teaching Excellence in the Social Sciences at Brown. Bil has been an active member of the Coalition of Essential Schools for over 15 years.

Acknowledgments

Books are interesting ventures. Although you have to work alone to compose them, their content and character are the result of hundreds of conversations, collaborations, ideas others have generated, observations shared, and scores of little things that transpire when you work with others. This book could not have happened if I hadn't been able to engage in all those things, and more, with my colleagues and the staff in the Education Department at Brown University. In particular, my fellow clinical professors, Eileen Landay, Larry Wakeford, Polly Ulichny, and Romi Carrillo have worked closely with me over the past five years, and their encouragement and support, as well as their ideas and generosity, are things I am most grateful for. The support of the department chair, Cynthia Garcia-Coll, and the tireless work of the Education program's administrator, Yvette Nachmias-Baeu, also made it possible for me to get this book written. And, of course, all the students I've worked with in the Teacher Education program have been instrumental in making me want to write this, as well as helping figure out what to write.

Friends unallied with Brown who have also made this possible by listening and supporting me over the past few years include my brother, John, and mother, Grace, along with Ruth Duell, Caroline Sheehan, Bill Legenza, Diane Dufresne, Kathleen Cushman, Ilene Kristen, and Antione Robinson.

Finally, I have to once again thank Bob Sickles, the publisher of this book, whose patience and support during some very trying times made it possible.

Bil Johnson
Providence, RI

Table of Contents

Critical Learning and the Promise of Democracy

by Henry A. Giroux
The Pennsylvania State University

I taught high school social studies during the heady days of the 1960s when it was possible to imagine that the "public" in public schools stood for something important. Largely unburdened by the pressures of privatization, the shame of commercialization, or the sheer vacuity of having to teach for the test, public schools represented to some of us the promise of democratic future and offered pedagogical opportunities to provide the knowledge and skills for students to become critically engaged citizens. At that time, schools were seen as a public good that provided students with the means not only for moving up the socioeconomic ladder, but also for participating in, and shaping, public life. Of course, at one level, this view of schooling was both complicated and burdened by its legacy of racial, class, and gender discrimination; moreover, the notion of democratic schooling was also undermined by its connections to a broader set of institutions that limited in practice its rhetorical commitment to serving the public good, and its silence about its complicity with those processes of inequity and power that offered middle- and upper-class students Olympic swimming pools, Advanced Placement calculus while simultaneously providing those marginalized by race and class with dilapidated buildings, broken toilets, and over crowded classrooms. At worst, public schools reproduced the power relations of the larger society and at best held out the promise of viewing and experiencing schools as democratic public spheres.

Times change. Schools are now predominantly seen as a private asset rather than a public good, teachers are increasingly being eliminated from the language of educational reform (except as test preparers), and students seem to be valued more as consumers and test takers than they are as potential critical citizens. On the national level, it is rare to hear legislators, educators, or parents talk about schools in ways that suggest that they embody society's commitment to a democratic future and offer students a space in which they can be honored, critically engaged, and nurtured with a sense of dignity and hope. Pedagogy is no longer valued for generating multiple, competing languages and practices in classrooms where different forms of learning can and do happen. Nor is it valued for recognizing how power shapes and is reinvented in the interaction among texts, teachers, and students. In short, I think it is fair to say that educational theories that pose fundamental questions about the democratic possibilities of schools as genuine sites of learning have largely disappeared from the national debate about the meaning and purpose of public schooling. Schools are in crisis and critical theories of teaching and learning seem to have either fallen silent or have been consigned to the dustbin of history.

In 2001, one of the major debates over public schools concerned putting the Ten Commandments on public display. Now in 2002, as I write this, the Bush administration has proposed that one viable form of educational reform is to reinterpret Title IX legislation passed in 1970 so as to encourage the creation of single-sex classrooms and schools. Against the new "common sense" of educational reform, teaching is not about processing received knowledge but actually transforming it. In opposition, to the profound antiintellectualism and corporate ideology that currently drive mainstream school reform, *The Student-Centered Classroom Handbook* offers a vision of teaching and learning in the secondary classroom that provides a welcome corrective in dire times. Although Bil Johnson's handbook is aimed at social studies teachers, it speaks to a much broader audience and offers insights that could be used by many teachers, administrators, students, and parents to improve both the quality of schooling and the pedagogical practices in which teachers and students engage. This book is especially important for those who share a common concern for reforming schools and developing modes of pedagogy in which teachers and students become critical agents actively questioning and negotiating the relationship between theory and practice, critical analysis and common sense, and learning and social change. The scope, boldness and eloquence of *The Student-Centered Classroom Handbook* is built around a project that goes to the very heart of what education is about and is framed around a series of important and often ignored questions such as: "why do we [as educators] do what we do the way we do it," whose interest does schooling serve, and how might it be possible to understand and engage the diverse context in which it takes place?

Bil Johnson is deeply committed to recognizing that education is about our hopes for the future and that particular forms of educational practice are central to creating modes of teacher work and student learning that expand and deepen the capacities of students to draw upon their own intellectual resources as a basis for developing critical skills and engaging existing knowledge claims. But, Johnson is not concerned simply with offering students new ways to think critically and act with authority as agents in the classroom; he is also concerned with providing teachers with the skills and knowledge to expand their capacities to question deep-seated assumptions and myths that legitimate the most archaic and disempowering social practices that structure every aspect of the ways in which schools are set up, curricula are developed, teacher work is organized, and student learning is encouraged. For instance, Johnson challenges the logic behind the seven- or eight-period day used in most secondary schools, a logic simplistically modeled after the industrial model of efficiency and control that emerged in the early part of the twentieth century. Johnson provides other multiple examples including the rigid organization and sequencing of the curriculum, the sorting and tracking of students, and grouping students according to their date of birth rather than their stage of intellectual development.

What is so crucial about Johnson's vision of schooling is that he sees teaching and learning as a political and moral practice rather than simply a technique. Teacher creativity coupled with adequate resources informs, rather than being separated from, strategies that make students the subjects rather than the objects of learning. Although Johnson provides an ample number of practices that teachers can use to promote a student-centered classroom, such practices are never removed from the empowering visions or democratic values that inform them. A student-centered pedagogy for Johnson becomes meaningful and transformative to the degree to which it provides the knowledge, skills, and strategies that enable students to become responsible for their own ideas, learn how to take risks, negotiate differences, become respectful of others, and think critically in order to function within a wider democratic culture. Johnson's teaching strategies reject both the industrial-management, hierarchical model of schooling and top-to-down pedagogies that treat knowledge as information that simply has to be mastered. In opposition to such models, he wants to create schools that share power with parents, communities, teachers unions, and others actively invested in the future of public schooling. He also calls for student-centered teaching strategies that promote a pedagogy of disruption and a culture of questioning.

As a critical educator, he brilliantly demonstrates through his critique of mainstream schooling that there is more hope in the world when teachers and students can question what is often taken for granted. He writes: "A student-centered classroom, by its very design, empowers students, gives them a voice, and makes them responsible for their work and actions. It also provides students with an active environment—and the activity is positive; it is about producing quality work, about engaging in rigorous intellectual challenges or real-world problems." It is within the sphere of unlimited questioning and sustained dialogue, that teachers and students can experience themselves as critical agents and learn how to oppose dogmatic forms of education which not only limit critical thinking, but also close down the capacity for self-determination, agency, self-representation, and effective democracy. By viewing the classroom as a space of dialogue, critique, and translation, Johnson offers educators a new language for imagining the mutual relationship between teaching and learning as both an act of critical understanding and competency, and as the possibility of intervention—that is, to paraphrase Paulo Freire, learning to read the world critically in order to change it. Pedagogy is always about the specificity of place and the outcomes of different struggles rather than an a-priori discourse that simply needs to be uncovered or revealed as an all-encompassing recipe.

Johnson goes to great lengths to illustrate how a student-centered approach to teaching not only is self-consciously aware of how knowledge, values, desire, and social relations are implicated in power relations, but that such relations must always be the object of an ongoing critical analysis by both teachers and students. At its best, a student-centered pedagogy should help teachers and students come to terms with their own power as individual agents and critical citizens. Students, in particular through this approach, should learn about the relationship between knowledge and the power of self-definition, and what it means to use knowledge to not only understand the world, but to be able to influence those who are in power and help to mobilize those who are not.

The Student-Centered Classroom Handbook is an informative book by a courageous teacher and critical intellectual. It will help parents, administrators, teachers, and others think more seriously about the purpose and meaning of teaching, and it will confirm what should be obvious in any democratic society: kids are the future, but to make such a future meaningful, public schools need to provide young people with the education necessary to excite them to become citizens. As Federico Mayor, the former director general of UNESCO, rightly observed, "You cannot expect anything from uneducated citizens except unstable democracy."

Introduction

This book is intended primarily for social studies/history teachers. But, to be perfectly honest, it is also a book that I believe needs to be read by administrators, school board members, parents, policy makers, and legislators. In a world where "testing" has become a national obsession, this book goes against the grain. It contends that *learning* is far more important than testing. It contends that active, engaged, noisy students who challenge assumptions, who make predictions, and who raise questions, are the true hope for our future. Silent, passive, sit-at-your-desk-and-"behave" students need to become a thing of the past. Learning is not about passivity and order; it is about the messy process of discovery and construction of knowledge. What this book attempts to present is a way for teachers to create curriculum that revolves around student inquiry and activity, a curriculum that demands that students become engaged and responsible learners and, in the process, enjoy it! Although this can look rather simple on the surface, the fact is, it requires change. It requires rethinking all that we do and the way that we do it. That is no small order. Most importantly, though, it asks that we think about *students first*, beyond all else. Schools, in their urgency for the efficient, in their desire to replicate industrial society, in their hurry to process their "products," have forgotten their true mission. It's got to be about the kids and *their* learning. So, this is a simple book, with simple suggestions, all aimed at helping teachers do what they want to do most: help their kids learn.

1

Why Do We Do What We Do the Way We Do It?

As we enter the New Millennium, a great deal of attention is being given to the "state" of education in this country. With the Cold War over and the United States' preeminence as *the* dominant power in the world, education has taken center stage on national, state, and local levels. For all the talk of "World Class Standards" and school reform, it is remarkable how little has changed—particularly in secondary schools. Just to provide some perspective, consider the following facts.
In 1892–93:

- ♦ The Model T wasn't invented yet
- ♦ A czar ruled Russia and Queen Victoria reigned over England
- ♦ Marconi's radio was still two years away as "wireless telegraphy" (*and commercial broadcasts were still almost thirty years away!*)
- ♦ The Wright Brothers wouldn't leave the ground for another 15 years

- ♦ Few knew who Albert Einstein, or Pablo Picasso, or James Joyce, were
- ♦ Freud was known in intellectual circles and Darwin's theory was far from accepted fact
- ♦ Most cities were lit with gas lamps and only the wealthiest Americans (or their businesses) knew what telephones were
- ♦ Long-distance travel took days and weeks by train and ocean liner, and
- ♦ The *American Secondary School system* was invented
  - ○ Four "major" subjects
  - ○ A seven- or eight-period day
  - ○ Curriculum was based on the concept that content-knowledge was finite

Put in this context, it is, to say the least, a disconcerting revelation. That little of the national debate around education raises this point, or the question *why do we do what we do the way we do it*, is at the heart of the virtual failure of secondary schools to educate all but a small percentage of our students well. The present system is based on a series of assumptions that have remained relatively unquestioned for over a century. Although some of these assumptions are *known* to educators, they still are not questioned in a way that will bring the kind of genuine reform our schools require. Richard Schwab, the Dean of the Graduate School of Education at the University of Connecticut, has said his state wants "progress without change" (1999, March 14, The New York Times), and it strikes me that this is exactly the affliction we suffer from in American education.

Although politicians, policy makers, and community and business leaders have all raised their voices about school reform and change, no one seems willing to genuinely engage in the difficult public discourse necessary to bring true progress about. So, we live with the same basic system that was handed down by the Committee of Ten in 1892–93 and act as if this basic blueprint is somehow a "nonnegotiable" in our school reform debate. In answer to the question *why do we do what we do the way we do it?* and in hope of provoking dialogue around that question, the rest of this chapter is devoted to raising questions about assumptions schools revolve around. Before we can consider how to establish a *student-centered classroom,* we must first examine what has kept this educational system from creating those kinds of classrooms (despite John Dewey's urgings) for over a century.

Questions and Answers about School Assumptions

What's the Educational Philosophy behind the 7- or 8-Period Day That Most Secondary Schools Use?

In fact, there is *no* educational philosophy behind the basic schedule most schools operate on. It is the product of an efficiency model grounded in the Industrial Revolution and the influence of Frederick Taylor in the early part of the twentieth century. Consider this: if this were the best way to have people productively work, why doesn't Bill Gates have his MicroSoft engineers get up every 45 to 50 minutes, move to a new work station, with a new supervisor, to start a task that is totally unrelated to what they were previously doing? In fact, secondary schools are the *only* place we will find this kind of system. It is, as many know, a factory, assembly-line, production model. It is not designed, particularly, for *educating* all but a small percentage who adapt to it and have a certain capacity to learn a small band of intellectual material in a certain way.

Although there has been some movement afoot to move to block scheduling, it is seldom accompanied by the amount of professional development teachers need to make such a radical shift. Changing the schedule doesn't necessarily change what goes on in classrooms (they still remain teacher-centered). Creating a schedule without some intelligent and thoughtful educational philosophy behind it is the core problem here. Because the original schedule (which still dominates the scene) was thoughtlessly unphilosophical, it will require time and facilitated dialogue among educators to decide how scheduling in schools could be designed to actually benefit *the learners*. At present, we have a system that is generally dictated by bus schedules, tracked classes, various union regulations, and a paucity of imagination and creativity on the part of those in leadership positions (administrators, teachers, and community leaders).

Progress requires change, time, conflict, and many other dicey issues that we often don't want to confront. Yet, no reform in history has occurred without moments of conflict and discomfort—dissonance is essential for change. Until we accept that, and put the *learners* at the center of the debate (not the adults and their interests), we may well see numerous changes without making any significant *progress*.

Why Is the Curriculum Arranged and Sequenced the Way It Is?

The Committee of Ten designated four major curricular areas in 1892–93: "Literature, History, Mathematics, and Science," and then proceeded to *recommend* that local districts decide the particular areas (biology, algebra, etc.) to be taught, and *in what order* those topics would be sequenced. To help localities make their choices and decisions, the Committee listed topics under the "major" subjects in *alphabetical order*. That many, many secondary schools still adhere to algebra-geometry-trigonometry and biology-chemistry-physics in that same alphabetical order is one of the great unquestioned assumptions about school structure!

Equally questionable, though, is that the four "majors"— essentially a holdover from mid-nineteenth century European university organization (by way of the *Middle Ages*)—is still the cornerstone of curricular organization in United States secondary schools. Despite knowing that involvement in the arts (music, painting, etc.) *increases* student achievement in *all* other subject areas, these are courses that are relegated to less-than-daily or elective status and are the first to go when budget crunches affect a district. Despite the fact that we live in a highly *interdisciplinary* world, in which we must engage in critical reading and writing, and use a variety of skills from all different disciplines to do whatever work it is we do each day, schools resist team approaches to problem solving or crossing disciplinary lines, as if doing so would somehow lead to the collapse of the system. With Howard Gardner's revolutionary work regarding multiple intelligences, as well as the continuing research into how the human brain actually functions around *learning*, it may serve us well to reexamine how we organize and even think about curriculum. As things are now, this area remains an unquestioned assumption—school *has to be* organized this way. The problems that this unquestioned assumption breeds lead to a number of other deficiencies, as we will discuss.

If We Truly Believe "All Students Can Learn," Is Sorting and Tracking the Best Way to Help All Students Attain This Goal?

By organizing curriculum as we do, and then packaging it in short blocks of time to be taught in, we create another problem for our students. Early on, in most school districts, students are sorted into groups (usually as a result of teacher observation or some kind of "objective" test) that will generally dictate not only their success or virtual failure as students but will generally segregate them from interacting with whole segments of their school community. Starting with reading circles in the primary grades ("Bluebirds over here and Vultures over there, please...") and culminating with rigid "accelerated" math tracking by the end of middle school, the fate of students is often determined by this form of school organization (for longer, more compelling arguments about this system see Jeannie Oakes, *Keeping Track* [1985], *and Anne Wheelock's Crossing the Tracks* [1992]).

Although there may be tremendous merit for grouping students with similar achievement levels together *for some portion* of the school day, it is ultimately disastrous to separate students the way we do. The creation of a winner-loser, competitive environment serves to discourage the majority of students in schools. Numerous studies have been conducted that show that teacher attitudes differ, too, according to *"what level"* student they believe they are working with.

That schools are not viewed as learning communities where the goal is truly "success for all" is one of the most distressing problems facing secondary education. The balkanized curriculum taught in short blocks to tracked students has managed to serve only a small percentage of "winners" in the system. Yet these assumptions remain unquestioned and are seldom, if ever, discussed in school districts. Until we begin an earnest public discourse around the unquestioned assumptions of schools, we will continue to thrash at school reform with few satisfying results.

Why Are Students Grouped According to Their Date of Birth, Rather than Their Stage of Development?

Of course, what supports the tracking mentality to begin with is that students are grouped in schools according to their date of birth. Step back and consider that. With all we know about developmental growth of humans, with all of our societal rhetoric about the importance of individuality, could there be a more arbitrary way to organize an institution. Certainly, it is convenient to organize schools this way, but consider what is lost as a result of this "efficient" form of organization. It precludes recognition of individual growth and talents; it ignores diversity at its most core level. What group of adults would allow anyone to organize them this way? It is only in the structure of schools that this form of arbitrary discrimination is adhered to *and* unquestioned.

Again, although primary schools have moved to multi-age grading (particularly in the K–2 years), we see this notion quickly fall away as students get older, ignoring individual differences for "grade-level" achievement goals (set by whom?). Ironically, by the time we get to high school we see an interesting contradiction in the pattern. In areas that require overt student *performance*—music and sports—it is not at all unusual to see multi-age grouping. What varsity football coach would deprive that gifted sophomore running back from playing with his seniors? What musical director would deny the first chair to the violin prodigy? But the academic areas have ossified into a system that accepts without question the assumption that it is somehow "natural" and productive to organize our schools this way. In fact, convenience, rather than intelligence, philosophy, or public discourse, determines quite a bit of what happens in schools.

Why Does Multiple-Choice (and "Objective") Testing Dominate Schools When It Is Barely Present in the Rest of Society?

The answer behind this question, of course, is that it that multiple-choice testing is the most convenient way to process large numbers of students (I discuss the problem of numbers and the assumptions that accompany it later in this chapter). Because so much of the curriculum in secondary schools is based on basic memorization and regurgitation (which essentially *requires* that classes be teacher- and not student-centered) multiple-choice testing is both convenient and efficient (particularly if a school has a ScanTron grading machine!). The problems this creates, however, are far greater than the efficiency or convenience it provides.

There are few places where people are required to have automatic recall of memorized facts (*Jeopardy*, the television quiz show, and Emergency Rooms in hospitals are the only two that spring quickly to my mind, in fact—and in the ER you generally have others to consult with, as well as electronic personal aid devices). Yet much of the determination of student "progress" in secondary schools is made by scores on these kinds of tests. Given Gardner's description of multiple intelligences, we know that these kinds of tests basically only tap into two out of seven or eight kinds of human intelligence (logical/mathematical and verbal/linguistic). Clearly, then, a large percentage of students, whose orientation for learning and developing intelligence does not fall into those two categories, are not well-served. This, of course, reinforces the tracking and grouping we see, the sense of who's a "winner" and who's a "loser," and all kinds of other problems inherent in that labeling.

What you may see developing here, as we examine these unquestioned assumptions about schools, is that they are interlocked. It is not simply that they are like dominoes that *might* bump into one another as they fall. These unquestioned assumptions have developed organically so that you cannot simply say, "Oh, we'll just remove this one from the line (like a domino) and fix the system." Critical public dialogue is essential for school reform in this country. Blather about "national standards" and "more testing" is pointless in a climate devoid of serious discourse about core assumptions that affect the daily lives of students and teachers. And change of this magnitude cannot happen quickly. These are issues that demand our attention now. Assessment of students is a critical issue—and one the remainder of this book examines in greater detail. To simply "accept" testing as it now exists is to continue to guarantee that most of our students not approach their potential as learners and active, productive citizens in this society. Dramatic as that may sound, examine these assumptions; go out and spend time in schools—day after day. Shadow a student for an entire day and see if the schedule, the tracking, or the curriculum are genuinely designed to excite and engage an adolescent's mind.

If Students Took Their Final Exams One Year Later, without Their Courses in Front of the Test, How Would They Do?

This question, which Grant Wiggins often asks in his work with teachers, is based on an assumption that if a student has scored well on a final exam—even an exam like the New York State Regents (in any given subject)—they somehow "know" the material; they have "learned" that subject. Yet, when I ask this question to teachers in workshops around the country, I consistently get the same reaction: eyes roll, heads shake, sheepish smiles unfold. We all know that the way most secondary schools work is that students spend about 179 days preparing for a three-hour Brain Dump in some gymnasium in June. So, if we all know this, why does it persist? Why do we continue to go through the motions of educating our students when we are relatively sure that one year later they will have forgotten just about everything from the year before? The power of the unquestioned assumptions strikes particularly hard here—and is at the core of what this book is about.

The way this system is designed—from curricular organization, to scheduling, to assessment—puts an emphasis on *input* rather than *output*. What's important in most classrooms is that the *teacher teach*, not necessarily that the students learn. It's not that teachers don't want students to learn, it's that the system is so entrenched in the "unquestioned assumptions" we are examining here, that people don't really know *why we do what we do the way we do it.* Like any good institution, schools continue to operate *because they are there*, not because they are necessarily fulfilling their purpose.

This is a harsh indictment, I know, but if we look at the facts, if we go into the secondary schools in this country (and, yes, even many of the independent schools) we will basically see what we have seen there for at least the last half-century. Teachers are at the front of the room, behind their big desk, often at the blackboard, talking, talking, talking, while students sit (often in straight rows, despite the fact that desks are seldom bolted into the floor as they used to be) listening (or giving the appearance of listening), sometimes taking notes (particularly if the code phrase "This is going to be on the test" is issued), and basically never seeing the connection between what goes on in the classroom and their "real" life.

For all the talk of "accountability" that is popular these days, there is little that focuses on discussing what *real* evidence of student learning would look like—other than more test scores. This is the *output* model that I would ask people to focus on and talk about, rather than how many more tests we need to give students to make teachers more accountable. A clearer focus on what students need to *be able to do* (rather than just what they should know) would provide a clearer path to the kind of evidence teachers should be collecting to prove, in fact, that students are actually learning anything in school. We return to this idea later in this chapter, and throughout the book, as it is a core response to the unquestioned assumptions:

Why Are External (State/National) Tests Necessary to Create High Standards?

Because transcripts and grades are basically unreliable indicators of student achievement, the notion that external tests imposed by states or at the national level has taken hold in this country. Secondary schools, do not, in fact, have any consistent standards—even within discrete departments in a building. If four teachers are all teaching the same course in biology or American history, the variance between an "A" in one class and an "A" in another can be quite striking—and even more so for "Bs" or "Cs." The culture of school promotes such a degree of autonomy for individual teachers that grading, and therefore grades, are unreliable. And therein lies the problem.

Because secondary-school goals are focused most often on covering content, there is no clear target for achievement other than that. This is one of the reasons that multiple-choice tests and the five-paragraph essay (more on that later) dominate the school landscape when it comes to assessment. Because few departments have ever sat down together to methodically discuss what it is that students should *know and be able to do* by the time they finish a course of study in that particular department, all teachers are left with is the input model of covering (then testing) content knowledge. The only evidence of actual student *learning*, then, are tests and essays. And then, teachers are basically left alone to determine what grades should accompany those tests and essays. This leaves teachers particularly vulnerable to the threat of external testing. Because grades will vary from teacher to teacher, and from school to school, only *external tests*, the reasoning goes, can truly determine if students are achieving "grade-level" status.

What this serves to do, of course, is bastardize curriculum even further. Teachers live in fear of these tests (because the results will be published in the local newspapers) and believe they have to focus their teaching *on the test* so that their students can score well. In many cases, administrative decrees demand that teachers prepare students for these test days, too, contributing to a growing sense of powerlessness and victimization within the school community. Aside from losing what might be valuable instructional time (so we can "prepare" for the tests) we already know that the students who live in the highest SES (socioeconomic status) districts will score highest on these tests, no matter what they are.

So, what's my point? Teachers (and administrators) need to focus on genuine and authentic goals for the students in their district and develop "Criteria for Excellence" in clearly designated skills areas (reading, writing, speaking, listening, research, mathematical problem solving, scientific investigation, etc.) and then focus their instruction and assessment on these areas (using *content* as the vehicle for teaching the skills). The goal would be to accumulate *evidence of learning* that is shared by students with the community and reflects far more about a student's actual progress than any test score ever could.

This is a complex and challenging task—and one I devote an entire chapter to later in the book. What is important to note here is that there is an *unquestioned assumption* about grading in schools—that teachers are autonomous but their grades are unreliable, and that's okay—that needs to be examined closely. And it is clearly interlocked with yet another assumption—that it is not important for teachers to know what their colleagues are doing.

Why Don't Teachers Know What Their Colleagues Do?

Another striking reality of school culture, based on the assumptions surrounding teacher autonomy, is that it somehow isn't particularly important that teachers know what their colleagues *really* do in their classroom. That is, the theory goes that professional practice is totally individualized and, once in the classroom, it is totally up to a teacher to determine how they do what they do the way they do it. There is little conversation *between* teachers about professional practice. The scant number of "professional development" days most districts have neither promotes nor encourages teachers to depart from a mentality that protects the notion that every teacher is, essentially, an *independent contractor*. This is one of the most detrimental assumptions schools, and the teaching profession, has bought into.

For teachers (and for students, too), schools operate around a mentality based on blame and punishment. The idea that another teacher might come in and watch you teach is unthinkable (or unthought of) in most schools. A visit by an administrator is cause for fear and panic in too many places. An observation for "evaluation" can make a 25-year veteran quake. What kind of culture/environment promotes this kind of thinking among its professional staff?

Teachers are the most valuable resource any school has. Yet, their knowledge and wisdom is privatized and even protected. Arguments arise over who can teach a certain subject ("Hamlet's mine!") rather than reasoned discourse revolving around what would be best for the *students/learners*. Professional cultures that promote genuine collegiality (rather than "congeniality" as Rob Evans notes in *The Human Side of School Change*) are not only hard to find in secondary school, but instead we see that the basic structure and history of the institution mitigates *against* it! Several other *unquestioned assumptions* grow out of this one, in fact.

Why Are Novice Teachers Given the Most Difficult Assignments/Schedules?

One of the most deleterious effects of tracking in schools happens when that practice intersects with the notion that "seniority deserves privilege." Simply put, our newest teachers are often given *the* most difficult assignments—often having to work with four or five "low track" (read unmotivated) classes each day. Consider the logic (if there is one) behind this: because teaching has always had a survival-of-the-fittest entry-level mentality—that is, if you can live through your first year you pass muster—the system has developed a completely dysfunctional (and illogical) pattern for bringing young people into the profession. What other business would give its most difficult assignments (or accounts or clients) to their most novice members? Wouldn't it make more sense to have those with experience, practice, and wisdom work with the students who are least motivated and most problematic? Yet, school after school engages in the practice of assigning to their newest teachers the hardest schedules. Surely, this is a formula for driving people out of the profession—which statistics bear out (we lose as many as 35 percent of young teachers within the first three years of their experience).

Teaching is an incredibly complex job that requires years of experience to become good at. Because society's attitude has been that "anyone can teach" and because the compensation for the job has been low compared to other professions (law, medicine, architecture, etc.) there is a pervasive belief that it just isn't that hard a thing to do. In fact, it is among the most difficult and stressful occupations to do well. Nonetheless, we have developed a system that does not provide for mentorship, that isolates practitioners from each other, and that systematically drives our best young people out because we have failed to question: *why do we do what we do the way we do it?* It is time to examine and reflect upon practices like this one and think about how to change this arrangement. It certainly does not serve the individuals or the profession well, and, as a result, is not serving the students and their families well either.

Why Are There Significant Numbers of Educators in Schools Who Are Almost *Never* in Classrooms?

Most secondary schools have an inordinate number of administrators, counselors, and other trained educators who are seldom, if ever, in classrooms working with students and teachers. Given that any experienced teacher knows that class size *does* make a difference (those who have taken a contrary position on this issue are invariably researchers or policy people who have never actually been classroom teachers), it is important for us to look at how we staff secondary schools in this country and consider possibilities that might actually put more adults in classrooms to create better student/teacher ratios.

In What Matters Most: Teaching for America's Future (1996, September, *Report of the National Commission on Teaching and America's Future*) there are several excellent models for restructuring schools to show how we can not only reduce the student/teacher ratio in a school but also *reduce average class size, reduce the average pupil load per teacher, and increase joint work time for teachers by almost 800 percnt*! (see p. 107 in particular). Of course, this requires restructuring how we think about schools and staffing. It also means we have to reorder some priorities.

When we planned the Francis W. Parker Charter Essential School (Devens, MA) our priorities were small class size (12:1 student-to-teacher ratio) and joint planning time for teachers. We also decided that teachers would serve as students' advisors (rather than staffing several guidance counselors) and we would try to keep the administrative positions to a minimum. The result was a schedule built around teamed, interdisciplinary classes that included a block of joint teacher planning time (about one hour) each day and a streamlined administrative structure. Although the leadership role has evolved over the first four years (from two lead teachers to a single principal teacher to a principal, with a dean of students and no lead teachers—all supported by a school psychologist and business manager as members of a leadership team), the school has stayed true to its initial commitments. But it is probably easier to start fresh, with no structures in place, than to change the existing ones we work with in schools every day. However, if we do not question the way things are (*why do we do, etc.*) then we will continue to attempt progressive reform in an institution unwilling to change. We need to engage in the naturally conflictual discourse that progressive school change inevitably generates if we are to have any hope of creating better educational communities for our students now and in the future.

So, although we struggle with generating the necessary controversial discussions, what can individual secondary teachers (and *groups* of secondary teachers) do? First and foremost, they can rethink their basic practice in the classroom, particularly if they are convinced that student-centered secondary schools will make a genuine difference for their students. They can look at their day-to-day practice and question "Why do I do what I do the way I do it?" Becoming honestly reflective about one's practice is the most important first step any secondary classroom teacher can make. This is not to say that this kind of reflection does not occur—Ted Sizer's *Horace's Compromise* was about a reflective teacher trapped in an environment of unquestioned assumptions. And there are many such teachers out there. But they haven't been given enough support to move into new areas of pedagogy—either through professional development or professional literature that is accessible and sensible to classroom teachers. The purpose and focus of this book is to provide clear and specific practical examples for secondary classroom teachers. Models are provided from real classrooms, supplied by practitioners who have struggled against the unquestioned assumptions and created more student-centered learning environments in their schools. As with anything new, it has not been easy and it has not necessarily happened quickly, but, as you will see, the work is clearly focused on student learning, not just teachers teaching.

The question that invariably arises when I encourage teachers to take the risk of using new methods and strategies is: "What if it doesn't work?" I have two reactions to this question.

1. It probably won't "work" very well the first time you do it. What does? If you learned to drive using a clutch car, what was your first experience like? As a first-year teacher, did you do your best work? When, in fact, is the first time you do something the best? Because schools have built in a "one-shot" mentality to their culture ("We'll try this new program for a year and if it doesn't get higher test scores, we'll scrap it;" "We'll go to block scheduling for one year, and if it doesn't work we'll go back to the old schedule.") it is difficult to get teachers to do what they encourage their students to do all the time: take risks. If you fail, you'll learn something from it. Pick yourself up and give it another shot. How can we expect students to exhibit these traits if teachers are afraid to model it themselves?

2. My second response to "What if it doesn't work?" is: that question assumes or implies that what you're doing now works perfectly—or, at the very least, serves almost all of your students to an excellent degree. We all know that that is seldom, if ever, the case. We're already starting to see that

students who frequently engage in performance-based assessments not only do not decline in their (multiple-choice, standardized) test scores, but often increase, particularly over time. So my question is: "What have you got to lose?"

By focusing on student learning in the secondary classroom, and breaking away from teacher-centered content coverage, we will be able to break those negative cycles that produce statements like "I taught it, they just didn't learn it." That's akin to the old joke about the surgeon saying "The operation was a success…but the patient died." We can no longer accept that what's most important in the classroom is the teacher's teaching. If that teaching is not focused on genuine evidence of student learning, if we do not shift from an input to an output model, we will never see significant progress for all the students in all our schools. My hope is that the examples that follow can provide secondary teachers with a resource for moving the focus of their practice more and more to student engagement and learning.

So, the rest of this book is like the clutch car alluded to earlier. It's a primer for learning for teachers. This chapter puts you in the driver's seat, adjusts the rearview mirror, and puts the key in the ignition. The rest of the ride is up to you, remembering that the first time through might not always be the best, but, with time and practice, you can become not only confident, but excellent at it.

Go ahead, turn the key.

2

Basic Strategies Across the Disciplines

Before examining specific strategies secondary teachers can use in their classrooms to make their work more student-centered, it is important to examine the philosophy and process used for making that decision. Although the notion of student-centered classrooms is at least as old as the teachings of Socrates, and was heartily promoted by John Dewey and his numerous disciples over the years here in the United States, it is crucial that teachers reflect upon *why* they should subscribe to such a theory. The basic model for practice throughout this century has not been focused on student-centered activity. Quite the contrary, schools have revolved around the notion of a passive student "learner" listening to the teacher and "behaving" properly. Here again, we must examine our history (asking, again, why do we do what we do the way we do it?) and understand that, in fact, schools have not really been focused on student learning.

Along with creating a model for efficiency, the secondary school, as it developed in this country, has also been focused on

order and **control**. This is ironic, in one sense, because at least one purported purpose of public schools is to create active, democratic citizens. Is it any wonder the numbers in voter turnout steadily declined over the last century? If people are told to "sit down and be quiet," if they are always punished for questioning "authority," (even if the rules they question are stupid or foolish), if people are part of an institution in which they know they have no real power or authority, is it any wonder that they do not become active citizens in a "democracy." Couple that "training" with our society's growing cynicism about politics and politicians and you may indeed fear for the future of true democracy in this country.

Beyond that irony, however, is an assumption about schools and young people. The assumption is that they can't, in fact, be given responsibility, that they can't be trusted, and that they need to be controlled by a fairly harsh authoritarian system. Given what we know about adolescent development—and its need to assert its individuality and independence during those years—could we design a more difficult environment for our students? Not only does it ask them to "sit quietly and behave" (for about five to six hours a day!) but it also requires them to lose their individual identity, voice, sense of personal power (and, often, space) and *submit* to an authority which almost never asks for their opinion, input, or ideas.

As Royce Van Norman put it in the February, 1966 issue of *Phi Delta Kappan*:

> Is it not ironical that in a planned society of controlled workers given compulsory assignments, where religious expression is suppressed, the press controlled, and all the media of communication censored, where a puppet government is encouraged but denied any real authority, where great attention is given to efficiency and character reports, and attendance at cultural assemblies is compulsory, where it is avowed that all will be administered to each according to his needs and performance required from each according to his abilities, and where those who flee are tracked down,

returned, and punished for trying to escape—in short in the milieu of the typical large American secondary school—we attempt to teach "the democratic system?" (47:315–16)

And we somehow expect students to learn "values" and "responsibility" in this same system. I raise these issues because I believe that student-centered classrooms address core concerns teachers and students need to focus on. A student-centered classroom, by its very design, empowers students and gives them a voice, making them responsible for their work and actions. It also provides students with an active environment—and the activity is positive; it is about producing quality work, about engaging in rigorous intellectual challenges or real-world problems. Much of the "discipline" problems that arise in schools have to do with students reacting to (and acting out against) a system that has imposed (in their eyes, "unfair") rules that they had no voice in promulgating. (Please do not read this as a plea to "turn the school over to the kids." The discussion here is focused on teachers in their classrooms becoming more aware of how to engage students in meaningful work and not pointless content-covering exercises.) Once again, what moving to a student-centered classroom ultimately does is cause teachers to reconsider the unquestioned assumptions upon which schools are based.

Constructivist educational philosophy believes that people only truly learn when they are engaged in "meaning-making" activities. That is, *constructing* knowledge for oneself leads to genuine learning and mastery of materials and skills. Student-centered classrooms are the inevitable product of constructivist thinking. Teachers, then, have to make a commitment to constructivist philosophy *before* they even begin planning student-centered classrooms. Asking the basic question, "How will students really learn _____?" is crucial to constructivist thought, and to designing effective student-centered, student-active classroom work.

To ask those basic questions, a teacher must be far more clear about what it is we want students to *know and be able to do* by the end of a course than the present system allows. Certainly for the last half-century, teachers had to make sure all they did was "cover" their subject for the year—whether it was biology or American history or algebra or British literature. There was no genuine requirement that **evidence** of student learning (other than some test scores and essays, possibly) be produced. Student-centered classrooms revolve around the *production of evidence of learning,* which means teachers have to think differently about how they plan their classroom and the activities that will go on there.

First Gear: The Process of Planning Backwards from Outcomes and Evidence

The first important shift we have to make in designing student-centered classrooms is to think differently about our planning process. Most teachers have been schooled in planning chronologically from September to June, working their way through "the material"—chapter by chapter (or the equivalent). This is why few people have ever learned much about American history past the beginnings of the Cold War, why biology students never get to human biology/anatomy, why literature studies never seem to include postmodern (after 1970 or so) authors, and why math "has to be" rigidly tracked to accommodate "accelerated" students. This model is linear and is focused on the *content* of whatever the course is. As a planning model, it does not take into consideration whether students **actually learn** the material. By virtue of being focused on content, the course necessarily becomes teacher-centered, the students become passive recipients, and little is truly learned (except, maybe, by the "high-track" kids).

Student-centered classrooms **start** with the question *What should students know and be able to do, and what will be the evidence of learning?* If we begin there, the focus shifts. It is not just about what students will *know* (content), but also about what they will *be able to do* (skills) and how they (and their teachers) will be held accountable for their learning (*evidence*). In this model, content takes a back seat to skills, to some extent, because **evidence of learning can only be demonstrated through this application of skills to content.** So, if we say that we want students, by June, to be able to read and write critically, to be able to do research effectively, to solve problems and think critically, and to speak and listen intelligently, we need to think about what content will most effectively provide learning experiences in the classroom that will facilitate student progress in these areas. We also need to think about what *it will look like* to see students producing that evidence of learning. In other words, what kinds of final assessments would be required to clearly show that students have learned the skills (and can apply the content) we have identified as most important? For example, if we want students to show how well they read and write critically and apply research through an oral presentation, we might design a final project or assessment that requires that they demonstrate those skills (a history convention paper presentation or a debate that requires source citations). If we know that our final assessments will include the activities described above, we also know that we have to be working on those skills throughout the year, so we can plan accordingly.

I recognize that this is a difficult paradigm for teachers to shift. It is uncomfortable. It may not let you say, "Well, by early November I'm usually starting the Federalist Era..." But what matters more: whether **you** teach the Federalists, or whether the students can actually argue, publicly, what liberal and conservative points of view on the Second Amendment are? If we want students to read, write, speak, listen, research, problem solve, and think critically to a much higher degree than they can now, our notion of **how** we plan must shift before we can decide **what** we plan. If teachers can begin to make this shift in their thinking about their planning, then the activities in the classroom have to become more student-centered. Once that happens, there is a wide variety of generic strategies that teachers in every discipline can begin to apply to their classroom practice.

Second Gear: Starting Small

Because most secondary teachers haven't used many student-centered strategies, it's a safe bet that most students haven't encountered them either. Therefore, when you begin to move into this style of classroom practice you need to start small, with simple activities that begin to teach students that the responsibility for their learning is in their own hands. What's important to keep in mind here is that these are simply *starter* strategies. I mention this because many of the methods below will be familiar to a host of teachers out there—there's nothing radical here. The problem is that these are only used as occasional "activities" with students and not as a stepping-stone to bigger projects that require more student responsibility, voice, and choice. So, though many teachers may have seen or used a number of the strategies described below, they have not been used as part of a bigger picture, as part of a weaning, if you will, of students away from the teacher's voice.

There are a vast array of student-centered activities that can initially be done by individual students, pairs, or small groups (though I'd recommend not more than four). The purpose and focus of these activities is for students to actually *apply* content knowledge they are working with. Many teachers are familiar with an array of graphic organizers such as Venn diagrams, mind-maps (webs), T-charts, and K-W-H-L charts. Before briefly discussing each below, it's important to think about *why* we would ask students to create these organizers. Quite simply, they can serve as a very effective assessment (formal or informal) of whether or not students are actually understanding the material they are working with. So, as a *starter* activity, graphic organizers can serve as an excellent first step in developing a student-centered classroom.

For example, any discipline can use a **Venn diagram**. If "compare and contrast" is a basic critical thinking skill we want our students to develop, a Venn diagram is an excellent way to start them on that path. By simply taking two items we want students to critically analyze and asking them to graphically represent those items in the Venn format (below), students will be able to show, quite clearly, their level of sophistication with this skill.

Again, Venn diagrams are *used* by many teachers, but too often as an isolated exercise and not as a conscious way of introducing more complex student-centered activities to the classroom. Teachers need to make students aware of this "stepping-stone" idea as they work on activities such as these. Demystifying **why** we do **what** we do with students will allow them to begin making connections not only within their classroom but even across disciplines!

In the example below, we can take a simple comparison, the North and the South at the beginning of the Civil War, and ask students to consider what characteristics were unique to each side and what they had in common. So, a student may create a Venn diagram that looks something like this:

Venn Diagram for Study of the Civil War

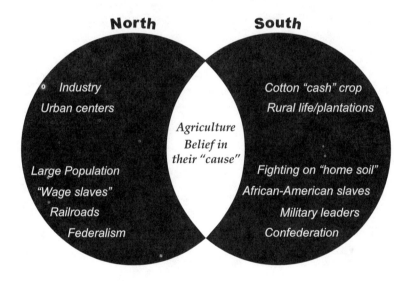

Students could be asked to post or present their diagrams and explain where they found their information and what they think it means. Any historical topic that is open to a "compare/contrast" strategy would work with a Venn Diagram, particularly when there are naturally opposing points of view. Getting students to do the work, however, and take the responsibility for making connections, distinguishing similarities and differences, and articulately explaining themselves is what makes this an ideal first step toward creating a student-centered classroom.

Mind-maps, or **webs**, are another activity that many teachers, in a variety of disciplines, use (though less and less so as students ascend toward 12th grade) but, as with Venn diagrams, they seem to be used as isolated or occasional "activities" and not as part of a larger, development phase of students taking control of educational material. Webbing can provide important information about how students process and organize information and can be a useful building block for teaching students important organizational and critical-thinking skills they can use later in the school year, as classroom work becomes more complex.

Mind-maps/webs can be used as brainstorming tools, organizational devices, content organizers, and process-thinking strategies. Starting with a "big idea" or concept in the center of a page, students can fill the page with associations, ideas, known facts, predictions, or whatever else the teacher asks them to focus on. The important part of a mind-map/web is that students **show** the connections they make between the various ideas and concepts in a graphic, visual manner. The importance of students not only making connections but being able to explain or defend those connections is a skill that most teachers and school districts would value in their graduates. Mind-maps/webs are an excellent *first-step* in helping students begin their mastery of that skill.

Using the North/South example again, let's take a look at how a mind-map might evolve for a student studying the Civil War.

Mind-Map for Study of the Civil War

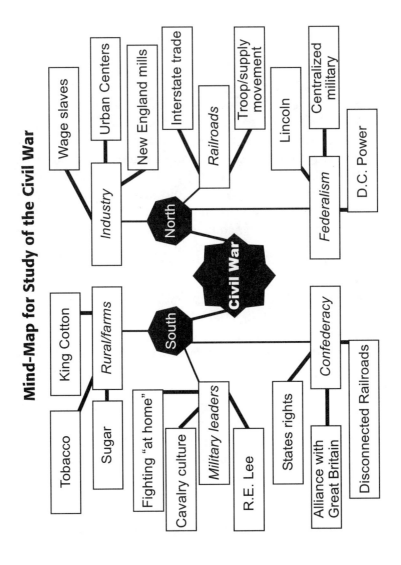

Even quickly scanning the map, a teacher would have some idea of what the student knew (or didn't know) about the Civil War. By having students share their work, present to one another, and discuss what they think and why, the students become more active and engaged learners and begin to take more responsibility for their own education.

T-charts are another, simple graphic organizer that teachers can use in a variety of ways to begin to have students more actively engage in processing content knowledge. The simple format of a T-chart (setting up a page with a big "T" on it) enables the teacher to find out what students know, how they think, what they can predict, how they compare/contrast, or any variety of activities that, again, make the students *active learners* who have to exhibit what they know and can do. As with the other examples, this is an excellent way to show students how they can provide **evidence** of their learning. T-charts can be used for pre- and post-reading exercises (Left side: What do you know so far? Right side: How has that developed?), for predicting (Left side: What characteristics does the element exhibit before heating? Right side: What characteristics does the element exhibit after heating?), for comparing and contrasting (Left side: What do Romeo and Mercutio have in common? Right side: What is different about them?), or finding out what questions students have about a concept or problem (Left side: List known and unknown variables and numbers. Right side: What questions or ideas do you have before working on the problem?). And, as with any of the other examples given so far, students can work on this individually, in pairs, in threes, or even in groups of four. The T-chart also invariably asks students for reflective analysis at some point after it is filled in. With a simple prompt ("By looking at your T-chart, what can you now say about _____?") teachers can begin to encourage students to actively engage in critical thinking and analysis, to synthesize information, and to evaluate ideas, concepts, and their own thinking.

T-Chart for Study of the Civil War

What we know about the North	*What we know about the South*

A logical extension of the T-chart is the **K-W-H-L chart**. By having students set up a chart about what they **K**now, what they **W**ant to know, **H**ow they will proceed to find it, and what they **L**earn, teachers provide students with a first step in developing higher-order critical-thinking skills (synthesis, analysis, and evaluation) by *applying* lower-order skills (knowledge, comprehension, application) to the content being studied. As an introductory activity, midpoint check-up, or final assessment, the K-W-H-L chart is a valuable tool and an excellent starter activity to get students to realize that the class that uses it is going to make them responsible and active learners. Here, again, is an example of how a K-W-H-L chart might be completed by a student studying the Civil War.

K-W-H-L Chart for Study of the Civil War

What do you KNOW?	What do you WANT to know?	HOW will you find out?	What did you LEARN?
The North had a greater population than the South.	Did everyone in the North oppose slavery?	Investigate primary source documents from people living in the North.	(To be filled in after the project is completed)
Abraham Lincoln was determined to keep the North together.	Did Lincoln really oppose slavery or did he just want to save the Union?	Try to find writings by Lincoln and others (at the time) and also look at historic biographies of Lincoln.	(To be filled in after the project is completed)
Robert E. Lee was a great leader and was offered command of the Northern armies, but he turned it down.	Why did Lee, a West Point graduate, feel as though he should lead the Southern army instead of the North?	Find writings by and about Lee, including primary source documents and biographies written in the nineteenth and twentieth centuries.	(To be filled in after the projects in completed)

If we have students complete a K-W-H-L chart like this and then share their knowledge and questions, students actually begin to shape the class's curriculum based on their own interests. The teacher, of course can coach and direct them in certain directions, but the students have begun to take far greater responsibility for their work. The K-W-H-L chart, too, is another valuable assessment tool for the teacher, helping appraise who knows what, how much content should be studied, what is being left out, etc. So, on a number of levels, the K-W-H-L chart provides a great deal of information while helping create a student-centered classroom.

A variety of graphic organizers, then, can serve as a first step in moving toward a student-centered classroom. They need to be seen as the beginning of a larger strategy, however, and not simply as "activities" that are used here or there simply as a "break" from the usual teacher-centered classroom. Graphic organizers are useful because they are easy to implement and they provide students with an initial opportunity to actively take responsibility for showing what they're learning and how they are thinking, and they give teachers a "safe" way to begin turning responsibility and accountability over to the students.

Third Gear:
Group Work, Jigsaws, Socratic Seminars

Although students work in groups more often than they have in the past, not all the group work that occurs in classrooms is particularly productive or effective. This is largely because it is not designed with a larger goal in mind—i.e., that it lead to greater student responsibility and independence for individual learners. Too often, as with graphic organizers, group work is introduced to simply change the pattern of classroom routine. In recent years, because working in groups has accompanied other "reform" strategies, some teachers have felt a certain "pressure" to have students work in groups occasionally. The complaints heard in these classrooms are common and widespread: the most able student ends up doing all the work; it takes too much time and we can't cover enough; too many kids slack off until the last minute. These criticisms are valid, but they point to a deeper problem. If you examine those complaints, what you find is a common theme in many schools: the kids are the problem. *Fixing blame, rather than fixing problems, is too often the cultural norm in schools.* It is easier to point out why something doesn't work—and particularly to blame the students—than to examine what it would take to remedy the problem. In the case of group work, teachers are not very good at designing effective group work, and this is a result of those same teachers not being given adequate professional development time and resources to actually learn how to implement effective cooperative/collaborative activities for their students.

As an incremental step in moving toward more student-centered secondary classrooms, effective group work is one of the best ways teachers can give students responsibility and make them accountable for their own learning. David and Roger Johnson have written extensively over the years on this subject and provide excellent guidelines for designing effective group work. (See Johnson & Johnson, *Cooperation and Competition* [1989], and Johnson, Johnson, & Holubec, *Circles of Learning: Cooperation in the Classroom* [1990]) Supporting their claims with years of research, the Johnson brothers provide teachers with an excellent design model that is the next logical step in developing a strong student-centered secondary classroom.

As researched and developed by the Johnsons, the five elements of effective group work are:

1. Positive interdependence
2. Face-to-face (promotive) Interaction
3. Individual accountability/personal responsibility
4. Interpersonal communication and small group skills
5. Group processing

> Johnson, Johnson, & Holubec:
> *Circles of Learning*, pp. 10–16.

If group work is not consciously designed with these elements in mind, teachers and students will struggle with group work and the complaints cited earlier will surely be heard. How then, does one implement group work that includes these elements? An excellent place to start is with a *jigsaw activity*.

Jigsaw activities have been used by teachers for a number of years and often are called *expert group* activities. In their design, they meet the five criteria for effective group work that the Johnsons have outlined. Imagine that we have a class with 25 students and we want to study different perspectives on the start of World War II in America. By dividing the class into five groups of five, and assigning each group a particular viewpoint to become "expert" on (Wall Street financiers, farmers, Japanese-Americans, African-Americans, working-class whites), we could design a group activity that meets all the criteria established by the Johnsons.

Basically, this *jigsaw activity* promotes **positive interdependence** by making each member of a group responsible for whatever material the group is studying. So, those representing the Wall Street group would need to read and discuss what their group saw as the pros and cons of entering WW II. Similarly, each of the other groups would have to do the same. In the process, examining materials the teacher provides, along with others the students might research at the library or on the Internet, requires **face-to-face (promotive) interaction.** Because students will reconfigure (hence, the jigsaw) with members from the other groups, **each** individual student must have the same basic information to pass along to other classmates. This provides the activity with a built-in **individual accountability/personal responsibility** component. Once the class reconfigures, explaining their point of view to members of the other groups requires students to use **interpersonal communication skills**. Once the activity is over, **group processing** can provide the teacher with valuable feedback as to "what worked" and "what didn't" during the activity. Checking on whether students chose important information, were able to convey it to others, and then, possibly retain it and express it on a test, essay, or other assessment, will provide the teacher with excellent feedback as to the effectiveness of the design of this type of *jigsaw activity*.

To express the jigsaw graphically, it would work like this:

Graphic Representation of Jigsaw Activity

First Phase:
Expert Groups

Second Phase:
Expert Information Exchange

In the first phase, the groups work on a common task, but **each student** is responsible for learning the material (teachers can initially structure this with specific outlines or prompts, to help students focus, etc.). In the second phase, **each student** is the "expert" for his/her group and must convey his/her information to members of *all* the other groups. This brings several important shifts in focus to the classroom that makes it far more student-centered. First, individual students become responsible for the success of other students. Second, students take on a "teaching" role with each other that requires them to learn their material thoroughly. Finally, though the teacher structures the entire exercise, it is the students, in small groups and as a class, who engage with the material actively throughout the exercise. In this way, a *jigsaw activity* (and other small group activities like it, which follow the Johnson & Johnson design criteria) moves the classroom a step beyond the graphic organizer activities, building on those initial skills, but requiring even more responsibility, accountability, and engagement from students.

Socratic Seminars: Making Students Responsible for Engaging Discussions

Another strategy, which puts the responsibility for the success of the class in the hands of the students, is the *Socratic seminar*. Initially developed by Mortimer Adler's Paideia Group in the early 1980s, these seminars are designed to help students delve deeply into text and become responsible for not only learning content but also developing speaking, listening, and reasoning skills. Because the teacher's role, once again, is primarily that of designer/facilitator, the ultimate success of the seminar rests upon the work of the students. In the bigger picture of creating a student-centered classroom, the Socratic seminar, like the jigsaw, is an excellent next step in turning responsibility over to students in a challenging and rigorous way.

Socratic seminars are a structured discussion designed to carefully examine a text. The term, "text," when used in the context of these seminars, is quite broad. A painting, a mathematical formula, a segment of videotape, song lyrics, the Periodic Table of Elements, would all qualify as "texts" for examination in a Socratic seminar. What gives the seminar power is that its success is wholly contingent upon student participation. Whatever text is chosen, students are expected to come to class prepared to closely examine the text. (In some cases, class time might be used by students to initially, individually examine the text) The teacher's role is simply to provide the structure, the design of the seminar, to have several initiating questions ready, and then turn the seminar over to the students. One "rule" of Socratic seminars is that student-to-student interaction is a primary goal. Unlike most classroom "discussions" (which tend to operate like a bicycle wheel in which the teacher is the hub and every other comment comes from the teacher before another student speaks), the teacher only makes a comment or raises a question *as a participant* in the discussion (after providing an initial comment or provocative question to start the discussion).

Although the focus of any good Socratic seminar is the text in question, the secondary purpose of the seminar is particularly important to the focus of this book: the seminar is an excellent way to provide students with an opportunity to actively engage in a rigorous intellectual exercise which they are responsible for. Any effective student-centered classroom relies on careful planning and design by teachers. The Socratic seminar method provides a basic structure that is easy for students to learn (and to use and reuse throughout a school year) and turns the responsibility and ownership of the class over to the students.

How, then, can teachers implement Socratic seminars? As with all else, start small. Choose a "manageable" piece of text. Start seminars as ten-minute exercises, slowly building up to a half-hour or forty minutes. Another helpful technique, when starting, is to use a "fishbowl" approach, in which half the class forms an "inner" circle (to discuss the text) and the other half of the class forms an "outer" circle to observe and critique the discussion (possibly taking notes on how many questions are asked, or whether boys spoke more often than girls, etc.). And what of the seminar itself? What are the "rules," exactly?

There are some basic guidelines that Socratic seminars follow (and I'm thankful to Dennis Gray, one of the original Paideia members for teaching me how to facilitate these seminars back in the 1980s) and, though they are not "cast in stone," they do provide a solid structure for students and teachers.

First and foremost, students must carefully examine the text. They should take notes, mark up the text, develop questions, and so on. It is imperative that *all* students have prepared the text before the seminar begins. Basically, students must examine the text for meaning, interpret it, and critique/criticize it. The first few times you try Socratic seminars, all students may not be prepared, or many may not be well-prepared—simply because they haven't had this kind of experience before. Once they see how much the seminar depends on their preparation and participation, their work for the seminar will improve.

Second, the seminar leader/teacher must be clear in explaining to the class not only *how* a seminar operates but *why* the class is going to engage in the activity. Helping students learn to focus critically on a text, leading them to understand that the seminar's purpose is to delve deeply *for meaning,* and that there isn't necessarily a "right answer," is very important. Keeping the students focused on the text is also an important role in the early stages of implementing seminars. This highly-disciplined approach to interpretation and critique is a valuable skill for students, but not one they will naturally exhibit, so coaching them, particularly in the early seminars, is highly important.

Third, the seminar leader/teacher must develop some opening questions or provocations related to the text that will "invite" the students to participate. In the case of a piece of fiction, the seminar leader might start by saying, "I'm confused about _____. Can anyone help me understand that better?" Or, in using something like the Periodic Table, the seminar leader might ask, "Why do we need to organize the elements this way? What are the pros and cons of this system?" In all cases, the seminar leader's role is to start the conversation (and then keep it focused on the text) but not to dominate the discussion.

Finally, it is important to debrief the class *after* completing the seminar. Looking at "what we learned" by examining a text in depth, what "worked" well in the seminar and what didn't (maybe several people didn't participate; maybe one person dominated the discussion, etc.), and thinking about "how we can improve" our seminar performance lets students know this will be an ongoing strategy in the class, encouraging not only their participation in the seminars, but allowing them to begin proposing what topics or ideas future seminars might focus on.

Group work, jigsaws, and Socratic seminars, then, are "the next step" in moving toward developing a student-centered classroom. All these strategies, of course, can incorporate use of the graphic organizers discussed earlier, thereby combining student-active, student-centered work in an array of techniques that are all designed to make the students the "workers" and the teacher more of a "coach" (an aphorism of the Coalition of Essential Schools). Employing these strategies builds the classroom community's focus on the students as active and engaged learners, and establishes work habits and academic focus that enables more complex student-centered activities.

Fourth Gear:
Simulations, Role-Plays, Debates

Many teachers, particularly those in history/social studies, English, and world languages, use simulations, role-plays, and debates as methods for teaching a variety of skills and content. Recognizing this widespread use, I want to emphasize the developmental approach I am advocating in using these strategies as part of a larger plan to create student-centered secondary classrooms. These are not simply those "fun" activities we choose to do occasionally, to give students a chance to get up and move around and, maybe, understand historic or literary perspective better. Simulations, role-plays, and debates, I will contend, need to be well-planned (and used in *all* disciplines) as part of a growing emphasis in the classroom that the responsibility for learning, and the accountability for it, rests with the students. When these activities are well-designed, they demand high levels of performance from students in a variety of important skills areas. Any effective simulations, role-play, or debate would require students to do significant research, to write and read critically, and to speak and listen effectively. In the process, if the simulation, role-play, or debate is well-designed, students would *have to* engage in critical thinking (interpretation, evaluation, synthesis, analysis, etc.) and some form of problem solving as well.

The teacher's role as *designer* is crucial here. Choosing content that lends itself to simulation, debate, or role-playing is essential, of course. But *developing clear guidelines* for students to rigorously research, write, read, speak, and listen are equally important. Designing the activity around an issue that demands that students think critically and problem solve is also vital to developing an effective simulation, role-play, or debate. What these methods provide, again, is a chance for the teacher to "coach" and guide work that the students *have to be engaged in* for the activity to be successful. As with Socratic seminars, students may not do this very well the first time around. However, if they've already had the seminar experience, as well as some of the others mentioned earlier, they will understand that it is ultimately their responsibility to make the activity a success. And, because these are highly public activities performed before the class, there is a level of obvious accountability built in to these strategies. It becomes very clear as to who did a thorough job researching and who didn't once the simulation or role-play or debate is under way. Later chapters provide suggestions for, and examples of, role-plays, simulations, and debates in a variety of disciplinary and interdisciplinary contexts.

Fifth Gear: Performances, Exhibitions, Projects, Portfolios

There is some overlap between these four methods (performances, exhibitions, projects, and portfolios) and the previous section's discussion of role-plays, simulations, and debates. Certainly, all the former activities are performance-based. The distinction I will make here is that performances, exhibitions, projects, and portfolios are more *formative* activities that generally occur over a longer period of time (than role-plays, simulations, debates) and have a more significant accountability function as their goal. That is, in creating a student-centered secondary classroom, the *arc of strategies* discussed here culminates with performances, exhibitions, projects, and portfolios. These are complex undertakings that occur over a significant period of time and totally require that students take responsibility for a wide variety of learning experiences.

Performances and exhibitions are linked, in their purpose and design, the way that traditional unit tests and midterm/final exams are. They are summative activities, in a sense, but are formative in their design. They are complex, in that they require students to apply a broad variety of skills to a wide swath of content. So, creating a series of laboratory exercises for the rest of the class to perform, reporting in a series of newspapers from several regional perspectives about a number of historical events, writing an anthology of poems or short stories in a particular style and genre, or composing a complex series of mathematical word problems for novice learners might all qualify as performances or exhibitions students would be asked to engage in over the course of a semester. It may be that these exercises are developed over time and kept in a portfolio, or are part of a larger project designed to unfold over a quarter or an entire semester. In all cases, the purpose is to make *the student's work* the focus of what occurs in the classroom. These larger, culminating assessments are the completion of an arc of developmental strategies that can convert secondary classrooms into *student-centered environments*. Within a semester, the focus of work, and *who* does that work, can shift from the teacher to the students by carefully planning activities and assessments that demand greater and greater student engagement. In the process, the quality of student work, and the monitoring of progress toward improved work standards, become part of the classroom dynamic that students are participants in.

The Arc of Student-Centered Classroom Development

This chapter has attempted to present a logical, developmental approach to creating student-centered secondary school classrooms. Using generic activities that can be applied in any discipline, the goal has been to illustrate how secondary teachers can use student-focused, student-active strategies to help students take more responsibility for what occurs in classrooms and become more accountable for steadily improving work.

In a more visual representation, the arc of this development would appear as is shown below.

Student-centered secondary classrooms can only develop if teachers consciously plan to make students more responsible for their education. This means teachers must plan to create these classrooms long before students show up. It means

Student-Centered Classroom: Arc of Development Strategies

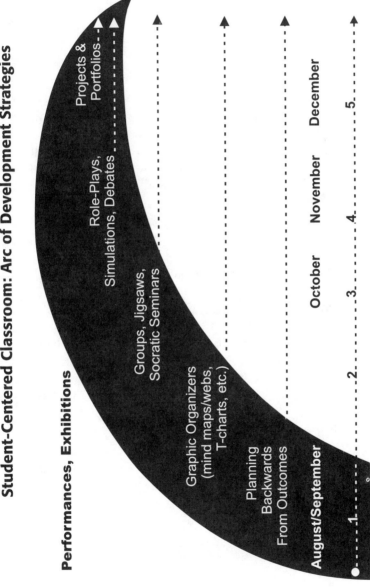

Performances, Exhibitions

Projects & Portfolios

Role-Plays, Simulations, Debates

Groups, Jigsaws, Socratic Seminars

Graphic Organizers (mind maps/webs, T-charts, etc.)

Planning Backwards From Outcomes

August/September   October   November   December

1   2   3   4   5

that the strategies discussed here must be incrementally introduced *and explained* to students as the school year progresses. The process of turning students' education over to students has to be a dialogue between the teacher and the students— and it must be an ongoing dialogue (which should include parents, too, but more on that later). None of this is easy and none of it can happen overnight. *But*, if secondary teachers have a genuine commitment to creating a system that produces *evidence of student learning* that is far more broad-based than the simplistic testing we have now, student-centered classrooms are a means to that end. Moving the focus of the secondary classroom away from the teacher and the content to creating learning environments—where students must actively engage in interpreting and critiquing work, where problem solving and rigorous reading, writing, speaking, and listening are the expectations for students, where genuine research is pursued, and public exhibitions of student work is the norm—holds the promise of genuinely creating schools where all students learn. But it all starts with teachers who are willing to break from the past, to question assumptions, and who are willing to design classrooms that operate in new ways; teachers who are willing to take risks, who recognize that the first time won't be the best, and who persist because, ultimately, schools are about student learning, student progress, and student activity. As teachers, we are guides, coaches, and designers—with the ability to have a huge impact on entire generations of students for years to come. But we have to be willing to take up the challenge of doing things differently, of getting behind the wheel of the car that you haven't driven before, and heading down a road you're not particularly familiar with. But the destination holds a lot of promise, and your students are looking for you to lead them there. Can you really resist that challenge? Take a look in your students' eyes as you head down this new path, and I'll guarantee you won't think twice about bucking ahead and learning to drive this more smoothly. And, believe me, they'll love the ride.

3

Kids before Content: The Social Studies/History Curriculum Conundrum

There is too much content to teach in social studies/history courses. Period. I'll repeat that: there is too much content to teach in social studies/history courses. Despite E.D. Hirsch's desire for "cultural literacy" (Whose culture? What *kinds* of literacy? Who decides?) social studies/history teachers on the secondary level too often consider *what* they are teaching before they think about *who* will be in their classrooms. This is a crucial, and often tragic, miscalculation.

The comment, "I teach history, not kids . . ." is sometimes heard when a social studies/history teacher is informed that a group (or groups) of students are not "keeping up," and that *who* the kids are should be considered. Maybe bombarding certain groups with facts, dates, and other information is not the best way for this particular group of kids to learn history (in fact, what group *is it good for*?). This misguided quote, which, I be-

41

lieve, is intended to reflect impartiality and "high standards," couldn't be further from either. That most students regard history/social studies as their least favorite (or among their least favorite) course(s) in high school is directly connected to *what* is taught and *how* it is taught. My contention is simple: you *cannot* teach social studies/history if you do not put the kids before the content.

Kids Before Content: What Does It Mean?

The concern too many teachers focus on, which invariably guarantees that all but the most motivated 10 percent will *temporarily* learn historical information, is on the amount of content and the lack of time to teach it—pure and simple *coverage*. This focus leads teachers to believe they cannot possibly take the time to learn *about their students* before diving into the rush of history. The result is disengaged, uninterested students who go through the motions of taking a social studies/history course and learn little. If you doubt this, give any group of students their social studies/history final exam *one year later* (as Grant Wiggins suggests) to see what they've "learned." Aside from that top 10 percent, most will fail miserably or, at the very least, show such precipitous decline that we have to wonder what the 180 teaching days were for.

That little or no time is *ever* spent teaching students the skills of historians or social scientists—solving real interpretative or analytical problems that historians and social scientists wrestle with all the time—is an issue tackled later. The initial focus here is on *why* students are seldom engaged or enthusiastic about learning history/social studies in our classrooms.

With all that is known today about learning styles, multiple intelligences, brain-based learning, and so on, it seems foolish for teachers to walk into a classroom just as teachers did a quarter- and a half-century ago and simply dive into teaching/covering content. In a world where the accumulated content knowledge *doubles* every two years or so, it is questionable as to what the point is at all. If we want to genuinely engage students in learning, if our goal is the *active* construc-

tion and production of knowledge and *not* the simple trans-
mission of information from adult to passive student, then we
have to consider who the learners are.

This is not to say that we need to be intrusive or intimate
with our students. But to be "neutral" and claim it is "impartiality" or a way to be "fair" is disingenuous. To not know
about our students—what part of town they come from, what
music they listen to, their left or right handedness, whether
they are active in sports, theater, the school orchestra, etc.—is
to deprive us, as teachers, of valuable information and strip us
of potential resources throughout the teaching year.

Certainly, the material of social studies/history is potentially geared toward creating active, critical democratic citizens. But, because the *material* dominates all, it seldom translates into students internalizing the lessons of history or social
science for use in the world around them. Because teachers remain focused on input, on *what* is to be taught ("covered"),
students too often learn little. Because the material is tested
with multiple-choice or selected-response instruments, and
five-paragraph "essays," students are seldom asked to provide genuine evidence they can actually *apply* what they've
learned in any real sense.

If social studies/history courses were planned backward,
with their focus on what we want the students to know and be
able to do, and what evidence we want them to produce to
show they've learned, we could more easily decide what content will provide the best route to learning. In other words, if
we say we want students to read, write, speak, listen, research,
critically think, and problem solve in their social studies/his-
tory courses, we need to then examine what content will best
engage students in learning to do those things. As it stands
now, every teacher edits the material before them—and usually according to what (s)he likes most and knows best. This is
why students in the *same school* can have vastly different
American history courses! Although the department may
agree that they will all "get to the Civil War by Christmas,"
Mr. X spends weeks on Federalism and the Constitution,
whereas Ms. Y uses the same number of weeks on Jacksonian
democracy and its aftermath. So, though all the students will

be "at" the Civil War by the holiday break, they have had very different course experiences. The problem here is not necessarily that the students aren't getting the same course, it's that the goal in the course ("getting to the Civil War by Christmas") only ensures coverage. Will either group of students be reading or writing better by the New Year? Will they know how to do effective research? Can they be given genuine historical problems and documents and debate issues? If none of those goals are clearly defined, and if no evidence of whether students are making progress in those areas is collected, then it doesn't matter very much what is covered (because most of it will be forgotten).

So, where do we go and what do we do in social studies/history? Aside from using the generic arc of development strategies, introduced in Chapter 2, what I would offer social studies/history teachers is a *systems analysis* model for teaching anything, any time, anywhere.

G.R.E.A.S.E.S—A Model for Analysis...and More!

When I started teaching in Bronxville, New York in 1987, I arrived with a model for teaching social studies/history that I had been using for well over a decade. No matter what the content of the course might be, I introduced my students to G.R.E.E.F.—Government, Religion, Economics, Education, and Family—as a way of examining any society or culture throughout the history of the world. Luckily for me, I got to work with Judith Oksner, whose thoughtfulness and creativity helped me improve my work throughout the six years we worked together. First and foremost, Judy suggested I revise G.R.E.E.F. to G.R.E.A.S.E.S.—Government, Religion, Economics, Arts/architecture, Science/technology, Education, Social/cultural values[1] to be more comprehensive. Having used this system for over a decade now, I can say with confi-

---

1   I have since met other teachers who use similar systems. In Stamford, CT, I was introduced to P.E.R.S.I.A.—politics, economics, religion, science, intellectual ideas, art.

dence that students will understand more about historical/social science problem solving, and engage in genuine critical thinking with greater confidence and understanding because of the G.R.E.A.S.E.S model.

G.R.E.A.S.E.S. is, essentially, a graphic organizer specifically focused on social studies/history content, thereby enabling the social studies/history teacher to introduce students not only to more student-centered responsibility, but also to integrate lessons with the other graphic organizing techniques introduced in the arc of development described in Chapter 2. By introducing students to this framework early in the school year (along with mind-maps/webs, T-charts, K-W-H-L charts, etc.) they will, at least implicitly, begin to understand that they are going to be expected to produce work, to critically think, to analyze, and so on. The instructor can be quite implicit about this, explaining that one focus of the course is that students genuinely engage in the same kinds of work that social scientists and historians do! By beginning the school year with students understanding that an expectation is that they genuinely *produce* work, that the focus of the class is on students *showing what they know*, it will be possible to move to a far more student-centered classroom as the year progresses.

Presented below is a ninth-grade Western Civilization course "mini-project" that asks students to apply the G.R.E.A.S.E.S format *and then be prepared to present their findings*. This was a project assigned to students early in the second semester of their ninth-grade year, so they had already been given a number of assignments using graphic organizers, as well as some assignments with role-playing, debating, and publicly presenting their work. That the project repeated methods used earlier in the course reinforces the idea that student-centered learning *must be recursive*—people cannot learn anything when it is only presented to them once. There is a need for repetition and practice (think of sports or music as examples of how people learn mastery of tasks). By February, these students were ready to *apply* graphic organizers (Venn diagrams, for example, and G.R.E.A.S.E.S.), role-playing (imagining they were a Renaissance philosopher, explorer, artist, etc.), and public presentation (performance/exhibition). By returning to earlier learned skills and adding greater depth, the abilities of students increases over time.

G.R.E.A.S.E.S. Mini-Project:
A New World Order, Renaissance Style

The Renaissance ushered in a New Age for Western Civilization. It was a world in which Western people (Europeans) began to perceive of the world, and beyond, in entirely new ways. Using our basic analytical model—the G.R.E.A.SE.S. format—we will examine the Renaissance from the points of view of the Key Players of the Age:

- ♦ Artists
- ♦ Writers
- ♦ Philosophers
- ♦ Nobles/Monarchs
- ♦ Explorers
- ♦ Scientists/Inventors

(The Clergy and Reformers will be examined in our next unit on the Protestant Reformation)
Your Assignment

1. Representing one of the Interest Groups you will "sell" the class on your group's Ideal World. In others words, from the perspective of Artists, or Writers, or Philosophers, etc., what is the ideal Governmental structure (and why)? The ideal Religious environment? The ideal Economic state? The ideal Artistic expression? The ideal Scientific world? The ideal Educational system? The ideal Social/Cultural environment?

    Explain/defend why your group's world is "the best." What makes your conception of the "New World" the most outstanding in Renaissance thinking?

2. Your group should also be able to define each of the following problems (from your unique point

of view, of course) that confronted Renaissance Thinkers.

a) What is (an artist's, a writer's, a philosopher's, etc.) relationship to the State?

b) What is (an artist's, a writer's, a philosopher's, etc.) relationship to the Church?

c) What is the Church's relationship to the State?

d) What is the relationship of Science to the Church?

e) What is Humanism? (What does it mean to your group?)

Written responses to #1 and #2 will be required and students should be prepared to orally present arguments related to their "ideal" world responses.

The G.R.E.A.S.E.S. format can provide continuity from unit to unit or even course to course. It is not meant to be prescriptive, however. If a teacher can think of other ways to *consistently* organize historical/social science material for students, (s)he should do so. As footnoted, I've seen P.E.R.S.I.A. (**P**olitics, **E**conomics, **R**eligion, **S**cience, **I**ntellectual **I**deas, **A**rts) used and it can actually be fun to brainstorm *with the students* about what elements of society or history we study that we can create our own acronyms for. At the Parker School, we added a "stutter" to G.R.E.A.S.E.S, making it G.-G.R.E.A.S.E.S because we felt the need to add Geography as part of the systems analysis. The point here is that teachers need to consider the kinds of vehicles of study that will engage students as active learners and then employ those strategies to get the most out of the material and the students.

A New Approach To American History

Most American history courses taught in high schools (public and private) follow a familiar pattern of chronological presentation, with teachers predominantly lecturing, assigning essays, and giving multiple-choice tests on facts. Although this system has consistently resulted in tremendous ignorance on the part of the American populace, it is seldom questioned. That few of these courses get very far beyond World War II or

the Korean War seems to be acceptable, too. Given the ineffec-
tiveness of these courses, why do they continue? Habit. Status
quo. Inertia. Lack of alternative ideas? What I would propose
is that we approach teaching American history a different
way. We need to start by asking questions, not focusing on
content.

What should students *really* know and be able to do after
taking an American history course? What *is* essential to know
and do? To pretend there is one simple and known answer to
this question is ludicrous, of course. That would assume that
there *is* a definite, known body of content that students should
master—determined by whom? And doesn't that only mean
focusing even more on facts, facts, facts? In 2002, I would contend we need to consider the following (re)design for an
American history course, starting with identifying *outcomes*,
designing assessments that reflect whether students have at-
tained the outcomes, and creating *essential questions* that will
drive our curriculum toward those assessments and outcomes.

American History Course Outcomes

Skills Outcomes

♦ Communication skills—reading, writing, speaking, and listening in a variety of styles and contexts.

♦ Data gathering, analysis, and interpretation
  skills—the skills of the social scientists and the
  historians. How do we put a story together and
  tell it? What is "the truth" about history?

These two skills areas alone represent a substantial curriculum foundation and a significant challenge for the classroom
teacher/curriculum-designer and assessor. Focusing specifically on readings and writings, levels of development in
speaking and listening skills, and *how to* assess student progress in those areas is quite substantial for a single year's curriculum. Add to that the skills necessary to work with primary
and secondary sources, as well as applying the techniques of a

variety of social science approaches to problem solving, and the core of an impressively challenging curriculum emerges.

Content Outcomes

+ The Constitution: what does it say and what does it mean? How is all of American politics and American political history derived from how the Constitution is interpreted? The role of the Supreme Court and its decisions. What is democracy anyway?

+ A Nation of Natives and Immigrants. Who is an American? And by what right? How many American Dreams exist and who creates them? Listening to the unheard voices of American history—then and now. And where does democracy come into play for individuals and groups of citizens?

+ The American Continent: how has geography influenced people, politics, and the economy? How does land create problems and solutions? How do natural resources shape values, create economies, and influence politics? Can geography effect a concept like democracy—and if so, how?

+ The U.S. and World Affairs: from stepchild to parental guardian. What role has the U.S. played in world conflicts—political, economic, ecological, and cultural? Who determines who the U.S. is in the world's eyes? Must the world be democratic— and, if so, why?

By looking at content curriculum in these broad areas, teachers can pick and choose those historic events that will evoke the deepest and highest quality student work. By driving the content through questions—some of which are presented above—the opportunity to cross-reference history (and other social sciences) with the present is always possible, creating greater possibility for student engagement and immediate relevance.

Attitude /Behavior Outcomes

The basic outcomes to consider focusing on as "attitude" or "behavior" outcomes are similar to those the Coalition of Essential Schools classifies as "Habits of Mind." Along with habits of persistence, curiosity, independence, and sympathy/empathy, these would be the ability to:

- ◆ discern viewpoint or perspective;
- ◆ search for or demand evidence;
- ◆ make connections between what has gone before and what we are doing now;
- ◆ identify if ideas, concepts, or thoughts are new or old—have we worked with this before?; and
- ◆ look for or demand relevance in their work.

Creating daily work and assessments that continually develop and reinforce habits like these in students is part of what performance assessment design is about at its core. The integral nature of curriculum, instruction, and assessment are best illustrated when considering the attitudes/behavior outcomes because these are the daily commerce of the classroom. How can we design student-centered work that will develop and reinforce these habits on a regular basis?

Designing Assessments That Embody the Outcomes

The next challenge is to develop assessments that will actually show what students know and can do in relation to the stated outcomes. Here, again, the break from the traditional curriculum-instruction-testing sequence is most obvious. We are no longer simply starting with 1492 and proceeding chronologically to the present, periodically testing the material covered. By examining the outcomes we want our students to attain, our assessments begin to take shape and the appropriate content necessary for achieving our ends emerges. Given the four broad content outcomes, for example, we can consider spending an entire quarter of the year on each, applying the skills and attitude/behavior outcomes accordingly.

In examining the Constitution, for example, we would have to consider what it is we want students to know and be able to do to demonstrate their understanding of how that document has influenced American history, how it still affects contemporary politics, and how it has been at the center of political development (and battles) for over 200 years. How could students exhibit such knowledge? Consider what students would have to know and be able to do to fulfill the following assignments. Also, note how, in the process of meeting the objectives of each assignment, students would *have to* work toward mastery of skills and attitude/behavior outcomes.

> You are a delegate at the Constitutional Convention in 1787. You represent the state of (x) (different students would be assigned different states). Your state has certain economic and political interests, which will be effected positively or adversely by the passage of the new Constitution. Prepare a position paper, which presents your state's views on the new document, specifically comparing it to the Articles of Confederation and defending the Articles or the Constitution as an extension of the principles of the American Revolution. Refer to the Federalist papers in your paper, as support or as spurious, misleading arguments. Make sure you are clear about your position regarding the necessity for a Bill of Rights: do you support or oppose the idea as essential to the ratification of the Constitution? Be prepared to present your state's case in formal debate, countering those who oppose your position and garnering the support of those who agree with your basic stance. If necessary, present other historical documents, maps, or visual aids that will make your case most convincing Also, write a persuasive Letter to the Editor of the Philadelphia Gazette to win public support for your position. Finally, be prepared to vote for or against the ratification of the Constitution after hearing the open debate on the subject.

An assessment such as this, quite clearly, will require students to meet not only some of the content outcomes specified above, but also a number of the identified skills and attitude/behavior outcomes. The questions that might drive this "unit" on the Constitution could be one like: "What is a fair and just government—and who decides?" Another assessment, which would address that question while meeting another of the Constitution unit outcomes, might look like this:

> You will be randomly assigned the role of a Supreme Court Justice. It may range from John Marshall to Stephen Breyer. As that Justice, you will have to write three opinions that indicate whether you are a strict or loose constructionist . The class will be divided into four large groups, each with a different set of three cases each. The strict and loose constructionists from each group (evenly divided) will argue their opinions on one of the three cases before the other three groups. The observing groups will have access to the Justices' opinions on the cases that have not been argued before they cast their votes, supporting one side's arguments or the other's. The cases we will investigate will include the Cherokee Indian removal case, the Dred Scott case, the Standard Oil case, Plessy v. Ferguson, the Warren Bridge case, Fletcher v. Peck, Brown v. Board of Education, the Miranda case, the Bakke decision, Roe v. Wade, the Koramatsu case, the Pentagon Papers case, and, of course, Marbury v. Madison. You may use other cases as references to support your opinions.

Obviously, students will have to meet all the communications skills outcomes, as well as many of the data gathering, analysis, and interpretation skills along with most of the habits of mind, attitude/behavior outcomes. All these are embedded in the content outcomes assessment and are driven by the essential question already mentioned: "What is a fair and just government and who decides?"

As this Constitution unit proceeds students would have to construct timelines, determine historical context, make connections regarding cause and effect, select appropriate historic evidence beyond the immediate assignment, and make numerous interdisciplinary connections to their work. Consider the richness of such a curriculum compared to the usual chronological survey most of us have lived through. Will facts be missed or omitted? Quite possibly. Will students have a far greater *working* knowledge of the American system of government while developing reading, writing, speaking, and listening skills and habits of mind? Most definitely. What is most significant here, of course, is what the students will *show* about what they have learned. The focus is on *student performance and achievement*, student progress in demonstrable exhibitions—a quantum leap away from simply quantifying students with a simple score.

Let's next consider the "Nation of Natives and Immigrants" segment of the curriculum. Given the growing concern about, and awareness of, multicultural education, this is an important content area. How might students learn about multicultural contributions in American history and how could they show what they know? Here's one possibility:

> The textbook company that published our book realized they made several serious omissions. They are sponsoring a "Volume Two" contest and we are going to enter it. The class will be divided into teams, each of which will write a Chapter to create "Volume Two." Each team will research one of the following groups: Native Americans, African-Americans, Latino-Americans, Asian Americans, Disabled Americans, and Women. We don't want to create a superficial "survey" about any of these people, though, so our chapters will be aimed at answering important questions that will reveal what your group decides is most important to know about the people you are studying. Include primary source documents in your chapter (maybe as sidebars, maybe as text). Consider the following questions to drive your research:

♦ Do societies or communities need an "other" or an "outsider" in order to define themselves? How has your researched culture played the role of the "other" or the "outsider" in America and how has it affected your researched culture? Consider—do any of these cultures discriminate against each other to create the "other" scenario? Is this a necessary component of community building? Can it occur without creating conflict or harming others?

♦ Can immigrant, aboriginal, disabled, ethnic, or feminist cultures assimilate to "mainstream society" without losing parts or all of their own culture? Why or why not? And how so, or how not?

♦ Why is it important to understand your researched culture in the context of modern American society?

♦ Who should we know about from your researched culture, and why? What significant contributions has your researched culture made to American society that we should know about (and probably don't)? Create a timeline that notes important people and events, to create the historic context for the class to consider.

♦ What do you think your researched culture's "American Dream" might be? What is their view of democracy in America—and how does that compare with your own definition, as well as that of any of the other groups and/or the "mainstream"?

Each team should be prepared to: present the class with its written chapter (complete with pictures, political cartoons, maps, graphs, or charts, as appropriate) and to give a brief (one class period) summary presentation about not only the chapter content but also how and where you researched your material. Individuals in each group will have to assume responsibility for focusing on one of the questions above and researching it thoroughly. Organize your groups carefully, making sure everyone is clear as to what his/her assignment is, when due dates/deadlines must be met, and what the quality of work is that the group expects to achieve. (The class will develop criteria regarding quality work, but your group should come into that discussion with ideas in mind—what does excellent writing in this style look like; can you find examples to share?)

By pursuing this research through initial, essential questions, students will have to raise more questions, developing their own role as inquiring researchers. Larger questions like "Can America ever achieve genuine democracy?" will raise deeper issues for discussion that will carry well beyond the classroom and also dovetail with the earlier work on the Constitution. Again, it is *the questions* and the assessments (designed to meet the stated outcomes) that are driving the curriculum. And, again, students *would have to* be *using* the skills described in the outcomes, as well as exhibiting many of the attitude/behavior outcomes, to complete this assessment successfully.

Over the past several years, many citizens, as well as educators, have expressed concern that students seem to have little or no working knowledge of geography. One way to incorporate that content area into a study of American history could involve assessments like those described below.

Imagine it is the twenty-fifth century and you are a real estate agent for Century 25, an agency that sells property throughout the Solar System. Your "hottest property" is the third planet from the Sun. People from other galaxies are interested in large blocks of land (not quite continent size, but substantial amounts of property—hundreds of thousands of acres at a time). Your buyers are only interested in the Natural Resources an area has to offer (mountains, trees, rivers, potential farm land, etc.). By researching the geography and topography of the Earth, determine your two "top properties" and be ready to present a convincing "sales pitch" to your potential buyers. You may consult with classmates on this project, but each person will be responsible for presenting a five-minute "sales pitch" with a one-page fact sheet on each of the properties (s)he is selling.

Although this assessment might raise some immediate concern from students—how do we know what the Earth will be like in the twenty-fifth century? What if the ozone layer is gone by 2400?—they can be instructed to indulge in "willing suspension of disbelief" and to consider the Earth as it is now—and maybe even in an improved condition if environmental consciousness continues to grow. Consider the *questions* students will have to generate to fulfill the assessment— and the research they will have to undertake to answer those questions! The teacher can then help the students focus on "macro" geography, examining the U.S. position in North America, with all its resources and how those resources have been used, abused, or even ignored. To examine the "micro" geography of the U.S. itself, they could do the following:

Each student will pick two states at random—they will be geographically contiguous—for this assignment. Your challenge is twofold:

1. Create a brochure that will "sell" your state to as wide a variety of interest groups as possible: tourists, business people (in a broad number of fields), families, politicians, religious groups, ethnic groups, and so on. Focus on the strengths of your states—their location, their natural resources, their human resources, their economic strengths, and their histories. Include any important statistics, charts, graphs, and so on. The brochure should be as attractive and informative as possible.

2. Be prepared to "sell" your states to a panel of outside judges. We will be bringing in members of the community, parents, school board members, other teachers, town officials, etc. to hear your

presentations and give you a rating (we will devise the rating sheet in class—it will focus on the importance and accuracy of content as well as the persuasiveness of your brochure and presentation). You will also have to be prepared to field questions from the class. Remember, other states will be competing against yours, so people will have done enough research on your states to raise "Achilles Heel" questions, trying to make you look bad and their states look good. Be prepared to defend your states *and* be prepared to ask tough questions (not take cheap shots) of others.

You will keep a nightly journal that will list your research sources and provide a daily reflection of what you are learning about the states you are researching. Your journal will also be where you record the questions you will ask of other presenters.

Although this assignment will initially focus students on natural, human, and economic resources states have to offer, consider the deeper questions they will have to ask about government and politics—as well as greater questions about the "United" states and the federal government. Is it feasible to work with a multilevel system of government (federal, state, and local) as we move into the twenty-first century? Should the U.S. divide into regional confederations to better serve economic needs and ends? What of those states that border Canada and Mexico—should they have "special" relationships with those countries above and beyond federal agreements? So, though students will be studying geography at one level, the depth an assessment such as this demands requires students to actively probe for more information than that which initially meets the eye. And, again, students would *have to* be putting the skills and attitudes delineated in the outcomes *to use.*

Finally, our course asks students to consider the U.S. in world affairs, in both historic and contemporary contexts. The assessments we could use to prompt their activity might look like this:

George Washington's Farewell Address (1797) and the Monroe Doctrine (1823) guided American foreign policy until World War II. Examine each of the following events and, in a well-organized research paper, explain how U.S. foreign policy conformed to or deviated from those policy statements. Conclude your paper by speculating how U. S. history might have been different if policy makers had conformed to, or deviated from, the guidelines set out by Washington and Monroe. Be prepared to discuss Washington's Address and Monroe's Doctrine in Socratic seminars.

♦ *Events to Investigate*—The War of 1812, The Latin American Independence Movement of the early nineteenth century (Simon Bolivar, et al.), the Civil War (relations with Great Britain), the Spanish-American War, and World War One.

Although this assignment seems to focus on wars, the students' research will have to concentrate on the concept of cause and effect and, more importantly, will have to apply the higher-order thinking skills of analysis, synthesis, and evaluation regarding U.S. actions in each instance. Previous units on the Constitution (role and powers of Congress and the Chief Executive), geography (who wanted what land and why?), and U.S. attitudes and actions toward "nonmainstream" ethnic populations would create a broad knowledge base from which students would conduct their research. In investigating modern U.S. foreign policy, students would be asked to do the following:

Since World War II, the United States has struggled with its foreign policy, often trying to be the "good neighbor" but coming across as "the ugly American." In teams of four or five, you will develop a position paper for an address to the United Nations General Assembly entitled: *U.S. Foreign Policy, 1945–1995: A Half Century in Search of World Peace.* You will focus on U.S. relations with regions of the world: Latin America, the Middle East, the Far

East, and Eastern Europe and the former Soviet Union. Your group must decide how to present the U.S.'s case: will you admit to errors and explain why they occurred, or will you try to defend U.S. policies with an explanation of the "greater vision" of world peace America has tried to maintain? You may want to consider presenting both points of view, depending upon which region of the world you are focusing on. Each team will briefly present its position paper as an introductory exercise to a class analysis of U.S. foreign policy over this period, in which we will share our findings and try to conclude for ourselves what U.S. policy has been over the past half-century. After the class discussion, you will, once again, select one area of policy (one region, perhaps) to write a "what if..." reflective essay, speculating on how things might be different if U.S. policy had been different.

The core of this assessment is somewhat "traditional"—do research, write a paper, have a class discussion, write another paper. Yet, there are some significant differences: the group work component addresses a number of skills and attitude/behavior outcomes; the research *requires* students to analyze and interpret events, not simply record them or list them; and the conjecture paper will reveal how much students have synthesized, beyond simple comprehension and application of knowledge.

World Cultures/Global Studies: The Model U.N. Approach

Another way to use the G.R.E.A.S.E.S. model is to incorporate it in a Model United Nations role-play. This can be adapted to any world cultures, global studies, or world history course simply by changing the components students would role-play. The basic assignment would be as follows:

Step One: You will be assigned a country in Asia, Africa, Latin/South America or the Middle East to research. In doing your research, you will be asked to focus on the following categories: Government, Religion, Economics, and Social/Cultural Values (particularly regarding Human Rights policies, etc). You should also create a map showing where your country is specifically located, who its neighbors are, and so on. Of the remaining G.R.E.A.S.E.S. categories (Art/Architecture, Science/Technology, Education) you may choose one you would like to research and report on.

Step Two: After completing your research and making your map, you will engage in a Regional Conference, meeting with the other countries from your area of the world. During this conference, you will not only exchange basic information about your countries, but you will also discuss your region's global interests. Also, during this phase of the project, you will determine which of your regional neighbors is most similar in its basic elements and political views to your own. There may well be factions within the region, and you'll need to know where you stand and who your allies are. The conference will finish with your Regional Group drafting a *Position Paper on Human Rights* for a United Nations meeting. You will be given specific parameters for the position paper after you have done your initial country research.

Step Three: Model United Nations meeting. This will be a multi-day affair, with the objective being to create an *International Human Rights Position Paper* that will be drafted, presented, and voted on by all the nations represented. Regional proposals will be presented first and then multinational committees will consider all the proposals and draft their own based on all the regional input.

Step Four: You will write a reflective paper on the entire process you have participated in, reflecting on your research, your regional meeting, and the Model U.N. experience. Consider what worked and what didn't, and why, and reflect on the idea "if I had it all to do over again, I'd… ." regarding the success (or lack of it) in getting your country's views incorporated in the regional and international position papers. Also include a short "What I learned" section, explaining what you now know about your country, the region, and other countries that you didn't know before the project began.

This project incorporates a number of essential skills on both individual and group-work levels. It is a straightforward jigsaw approach, requiring students to be responsible for individual work that then has significance to greater group goals. It enables the teacher to monitor individual student research as well as coach group work as it progresses. It is also a very adaptable framework, as presented above, for teaching world cultures or global studies. A teacher can easily list *which* countries in each region the students will research. In that sense, the project becomes quite adaptable to current events. If certain countries in Latin/South America are "hot topics" in the news, those are the ones that can be researched. The same would be true for any of the other regions.

This project can also be adapted to teach historic material as well. Whether it's Medieval or Renaissance Europe, Feudal Japan, or Imperial China, the role-play can be adapted to provincial regions, blocs of countries, principalities, etc. Students would then do individual historical research and meet in groups to consider some common issue (the Magna Carta, opening/closing Chinese trade, the Protestant Reformation, etc.). They would represent a variety of perspectives and develop the same critical-thinking, problem-solving, and public-presentation skills (as well as reading, writing, and research skills) that are developed with the Model U.N. simulation, while actively using the G.R.E.A.S.E.S. system.

It's All About the Kids

In the examples presented here, the focus has been on making sure that students *actively learn*. Given the volume of material social studies/history encompasses, it is impossible to transmit tons of content and expect high school students to retain it all. What has been presented here are methods for engaging students actively in their learning, and making them responsible for mastering (or at least attempting to master) content through the application of those skills that will transfer to other learning. Therefore, all our planning has to be focused on *who* our students are, *what* it is they need to know and be able to do, and then *clearly defining* our outcomes. Although I have consistently used the examples of reading, writing, speaking, listening, research, critical thinking, and problem solving as the basic skills we can focus on, I want to emphasize that our outcomes/objectives must be far more precise. That is, we have to *very specifically* identify what kinds of writing skills we want our students to master. Should they know how to write an editorial or op-ed piece? Do we want them to be able to write an historic paper worthy of presenting at a history conference? In what ways do we want them to present an argument and support it with evidence? These questions, and others like them, must run through the mind of the curriculum designer so that the students have clear targets. They need to know, from day one, what is expected of them and where they are going. In fact, when you can present students with clear objectives, you will less and less hear the question, "Why are we doing this?" By focusing on skills first, and clear, well-defined skills, the social studies/history teacher can then decide which areas of content can most suitably (and actively) help students learn. In the process, students will actually retain more content—and for a far greater period of time!

The Challenge

In a period when standardized testing is dominating not only the headlines but state departments of education as well, it is genuinely a challenge for teachers to put *real learning* on their front burner. The fallacy is that the situation is an either/or one. The next chapter attempts to disprove that either/or mentality. Social studies/history teachers need not be overwhelmed by the content of their courses, particularly not at the expense of creating a lively, active curriculum in which their students will consistently present the products of their learning. A curriculum that puts the students at the center and uses skills and content instruction to further authentic learning is one that will serve all our students best. It is one that also brings out the creativity in teachers and translates into engaged and lively classrooms where we can see what our students are learning. There are always reasons for backing down from a challenge like this, far too many to enumerate here. But are those reasons good enough to deny students the chance to actively learn? Are they good enough reasons to deny kids the opportunity to learn essential skills? That's the challenge and those are the questions—where do you stand?

4

In the Face of Standards and Testing: Strategies and Methods

As mentioned at the end of the last chapter, the onslaught of "standards" accompanied by batteries of standardized tests has painted many people into a corner that educational issues are often relegated to: the either/or corner. The argument is, of course, "If we're going to prepare kids to score well (or at least better) on *the tests*, we have to cover the material to make sure they're ready!" The point that's missed here is a simple one. If our knowledge of history is accurate at all, we know several things about this kind of test preparation: kids' scores will accord with what we already know about their basic literacy/numeracy skills, and kids from more affluent school districts will score highest whereas kids from poor districts will score lowest. The irony that is missed, I think, is that the kids from those more affluent districts often take Stanley Kaplan or Princeton Review prep courses where they are not taught or drilled on content but learn *test-taking strategies*. I bring this up because I believe if teachers faced with administrative threats of "higher scores or else" think about what they need to do, they may see that the "either/or" corner is not where they have to go. What I outline in this chapter are methods and strategies for improving student skills in critical thinking and problem solving—even as the students work on developing stronger literacy skills. And I show that you can employ a very student-centered, student-active curriculum while not sacrificing preparing your students for the tests they will have to take.

Strategies and Methods: Active Learning in the Secondary Classroom

Some of the methods discussed here have been referred to in earlier chapters without reference to *specific* application (the Socratic seminars explanation, for example, doesn't include references to specific texts one might use). What I hope to show in what follows are some very practical ways to engage students in an active, project-oriented classroom while still making sure that material is "covered" and students are challenged to improve their literacy skills on a consistent basis. As in the last chapter, specific examples will be presented so that the practicality of implementing a student-centered secondary curriculum will be clear.

The examples below demonstrate how cooperative/collaborative learning, Socratic seminars, jigsaws, graphic organizers, simulations, projects, and exhibitions can all be used in ways that put the student at the center of the work, making him/her responsible for his/her own learning.

The Conference in Rico Futuro

Whereas the last chapter presented an example of how one might use a role-play for students to learn about the United States' Constitutional Convention, what follows here is a more elaborate simulation that provides more depth in researching the issues surrounding the creation of the U.S. Constitution.

This simulation, which could occur over a period as short as three days, but could also take a week or two (depending on the teacher's long-term design), is designed to create its own world in the classroom, where students are solving the problems of a mythic nation set on the west coast of South America. By getting students to suspend disbelief and simply participate in a "game," a great deal of active learning occurs, even though the students may not recognize it while its occurring.

Setting the Table

This simulation works best at the very beginning of the school year and, though it is designed for an American history class, it could be adapted for any social studies/history course that is going to investigate the creation of a new Constitution in any country at any point in history. For example, an adapted version of this (or a follow-up project) might be applied to the creation of a new Constitution in Afghanistan or Palestine. So, although this example is designed for a rather traditional American history course, the possibilities for its use are limited only by the creativity of the teacher using it.

The basic setup is that students are told they are going to participate in a Constitutional Convention in a mythic South American country at the end of the twentieth century. Each student will be given a role as a delegate from a particular province (trying to evenly divide up the class for the proceedings). Once the students have been assigned a role, they are given a *"Delegate's Packet"* of materials (all of which follows). We review what is in the packet and what our time line for the convention will be and we ask the students to begin thinking about what their positions will be on the various issues.

The Delegate's Packet contains "The Revolutionary Principles of Rico Futuro" (which is, with little deviation, The U.S. Articles of Confederation), the History of Rico Futuro (which parallels U.S. history prior to the Constitutional Convention), a Conference Agenda and Schedule, as well as Conference rules (which are basically copied from Madison's notes), a specific assignment sheet with tasks and responsibilities, two maps of Rico Futuro, a set of "Province Profiles" (where the names of the Provinces are actually word scrambles of some of the original U.S. colonies/states), and a sheet with the 1985 census and economic indebtedness figures (all based on the U.S. population and debt in 1787). Once students are familiar with these materials and their own role, a chairperson and convention secretary are appointed and the "game" can begin.

With this setup, the teacher's role quite naturally becomes one of a coach, because the students have the responsibility of drafting a document within several days. In the process, the teacher can assign any number of activities that have been mentioned earlier. There are numerous ways students could use graphic organizers; the division of students into committees or subcommittees would make various kinds of group work possible; and jigsaws could be used as well. The Revolutionary Principles could be used as the text for a Socratic seminar. Depending on the time the teacher decides is necessary, as well as the depth the teacher wants the students to probe, the simulation can be adapted in any variety of ways to hone literacy, critical-thinking, and problem-solving skills, while conveying a great deal about historic content. After examining the content of the simulation, the possibilities for follow-up student-centered work are discussed. For now, though, on to Rico Futuro!

Conference in Rico Futuro

The Present Situation

♦ Five years ago, the citizens of Rico Futuro won their independence from their colonial rulers after a bloody guerilla war that lasted almost a decade.

♦ Like most Third World countries, Rico Futuro is primarily an agrarian society, with little technology and industry. The economy of Rico Futuro is based primarily on subsistence farming, fishing, and the export of raw materials. They import the bulk of the manufactured goods they need, etc.

♦ During and after the Revolution, Rico Futuro was run by a Council of Representatives elected from the eleven provinces of the country. The Council raised money for the guerillas during the revolution against Grande Imperio and eventually negotiated a treaty of independence. Since the Revolution's end, however, the government has faltered in guiding Rico Futuro, particularly economically.

♦ Presently, most of the "business" of the country, and its governance, is controlled by the eleven local, provincial governments—in some cases quite effectively; in others, less so.

♦ Rico Futuro is a 1000-mile-long country along the Pacific Ocean, extending 200 miles inland to the Andes Mountains. The new nation also owns a tract of jungle and wilderness territory extending into the Amazon region bordering western Brazil—a prize of the revolutionary victory. Many of the provincial governments have already laid claim to sections of the Eastern Territory, hoping to expand and improve their economies (see Map 1). Disputes over claimed territories have already arisen between the provinces.

♦ The inhabitants of Rico Futuro are from varied heritages, paralleling their 200-year colonial settlement. Among their citizens, there are people of German, French, Italian and Portuguese descent—and even *some* from England and America! There is a large, subservient native American population, the Incas—conquered years ago by the early settlers. They have, in some cases, mixed with settlers, creating a Mestizo population. The Indians and Mestizos are primarily common laborers and did not participate in the revolution.

♦ As happens after most revolutions, there has been an increasing economic recession, inflation, devaluation of currency, and the threat of external invasion from neighboring countries to the north, south and east, as well as foreign intrigue and "interference" from superpowers arming and supplying counter-revolutionaries in the jungles.

The Revolutionary Principles of the Provinces of Rico Futoro

The free and independent Provinces of Rico Futuro resolve to create a firm league of friendship now and forever known as the Unified Provinces of Rico Futuro.

Article One: Each Province retains its sovereignty, freedom, independence, and all powers that are not specifically delegated in this document to the Unified government of Rico Futuro.

Article Two: The Provinces declare here that they have entered a firm league of friendship with each other for common defense, the security of their liberties and their mutual welfare, promising to assist each other against all force or attacks made against them on account of nationality, religion, economics, political beliefs, or any other reason whatsoever.

Article Three: This document establishes the creation of a Chamber of Legislators—the Gobierno Cuarto—with each Province Representative who will have one vote, equal to all others. The Gobierno Cuarto will have the power to:

1. Declare war and peace.
2. Fix Provincial quotas of men and monies for the National Army.
3. Make treaties and alliances.
4. Decide disputes and fix boundaries between Provinces.
5. Admit new Provinces from the Eastern Territory.
6. Request operating expenses from Provincial Councils, according to needs and ability to pay.
7. Establish Post Offices and other public facilities according to their need.
8. Elect a Chairman from the assembled Representatives to conduct meetings and represent the country in foreign affairs, according to the writ-

ten dictates of the Gobierno Cuarto and the Provincial Councils.

Article Four: All laws will require a Seven-Vote majority to
pass.

Article Five: Any Amendment to the Revolutionary Principles
requires a Unanimous Vote of the Gobierno Cuarto.

May 19, 1975

The History of Rico Futuro

Originally "discovered" in 1549 (the native Incans already
knew it was there, of course), Rico Futuro was a land rich in resources. The major colony founded by Grande Imperio (a
Mediterranean island nation between Spain and Sicily with,
quite naturally, a powerful navy), its original colonists were of
Spanish and Italian ancestry. By 1600, however, the vast
coastal colony had drawn settlers from Portugal and England,
too. Later in the century, a fairly large colony of German Prot-
estants also emigrated to the colony.

Initially settled along the coast, Grande Imperio began establishing provincial governments run by governors sent
from the mother country. A thriving import/export trading
economy developed in Rico Futuro, supplying Grande
Imperio with bananas, citrus fruits, coffee, tobacco, timber,
and cocoa—and receiving manufactured goods in return. The
native Incan culture was totally conquered by 1700 and was
used as a slave-labor force until 1820, the year known as the
Year of Rebellion.

In 1820, the northern provinces attempted to break away
from Grande Imperio and establish their independence, but
lack of support from the Southern provinces, the Eastern jungle pioneers, the Incans, and any foreign nations doomed the
revolt to failure. Grande Imperio responded by establishing a
harsh military-dominated government, abolishing any local
legislature, heavily taxing the colony, and totally abolishing
local voting rights. Grande Imperio maintained this rigid and,
to the colonists, brutal, control until the end of World War II in
1945.

The post-war era brought almost constant conflict to Rico Futuro, culminating in the Revolution of 1975. After a decade-long bloody struggle, Rico Futuro won its total independence in 1985 and began operating the independent government that is now being considered for revision.

Current Problems in Rico Futuro to Be Considered at the Conference

- ◆ Governments/Politics
  - ◦ Questions about the power of the government.
  - ◦ The relationship of the central government to the provincial ones
  - ◦ More power to the central government?
  - ◦ Representation? More than one vote per province?
- ◆ Social/cultural
  - ◦ The Incans: should they become citizens?
  - ◦ Religion's influence on the government?
  - ◦ Promotion of arts/sciences: Should the government fund research, etc.?
  - ◦ Public schools, colleges, etc.?
- ◆ Economics
  - ◦ More control/power for the central government?
  - ◦ Development of industry and banking?
  - ◦ Payment of debts?

Conference Agenda/Schedule and Rules

Agenda/Schedule

Day One _____

- ◆ Review the current government (homework)
- ◆ The Legislative Body
  - ○ Suggested revisions: terms of office, powers, a second house?
  - ○ Debate proposals
  - ○ Resolution: vote/write

Day Two _____

- ◆ Creation of an Executive Department
  - ○ Yes or no? Why/why not?
  - ○ If yes: powers? limitations?
  - ○ Debate/resolve/write

Day Three _____

- ◆ Creation of a Judicial Branch
  - ○ Create more than local, provincial courts? Why/why not?
  - ○ If yes: define powers/limitations, etc.
  - ○ Debate/resolve/write

Day Four _____

- ◆ Amending Process
  - ○ Can this document be changed? Yes/No
  - ○ If yes: how? What changes might occur, etc.?
  - ○ Debate/resolve/write

Day Five _____

- ◆ Write a final draft of revisions and vote on it.

Conference Rules

1. A chairperson will be selected to oversee the conference.

2. A secretary will be selected and keep daily notes.

3. All delegates will keep notes and journals.

4. Delegates will be recognized by the chair to speak and must rise and present their proposals. While a delegate is speaking no other delegate may speak, pass notes, shuffle papers, read a book, etc.

5. Members will raise their hands to be recognized and the chairperson will create a speaker's list, to promote orderly debate.

6. No delegate will speak more than twice (unless the chairperson makes an exception) until *every* province has been heard from on each proposal.

7. Motions will be made and must be seconded. The motion will be read aloud by the secretary before debate commences. Any motion may be withdrawn by the person(s) making it at any time.

8. When a motion is being debated, no other motion will be entertained unless it is to amend the one under discussion.

9. A question that is complex may be broken into sections for discussion and divided into separate issues to be voted on one at a time.

10. All issues on the agenda will be resolved in the day allotted them and *cannot* be carried over to the next day except for exceptional circumstances or by unanimous vote of the conference.

11. Committees may be formed on a voluntary or voted basis, if the conference feels it is necessary to further define an issue. Committees may be formed to write resolutions into draft form.

12. A delegate may be called to order by another member, appealing to the chairperson, for speaking out of turn or for any other form of improper conduct.

13. The conference will only be adjourned after all the business on that day's agenda has been completed.

Conference in Rico Futuro: Your Mission

The present government—the Provincial Council—has called for a conference to revise the Revolutionary Principles (the Rico Futuro Constitution) so as to better cope with the problems of 1990—none of which seemed to exist in 1975, when the Revolution began and the Revolutionary Principles were first written.

Your Task

You have been selected as a Provincial Delegate to the Revolutionary Principles Conference in the capital city of El Dorado. Your objective is to revise the Revolutionary Principles to cope better with the problems of the day—and the future.

Delegate's Materials

- A copy of the Revolutionary Principles
- Two maps of Rico Futuro
- A profile of the provinces
- A thumbnail sketch of each province's characteristics
- A brief history of Rico Futuro
- Conference Rules, Agenda, and Schedule

Delegate's Responsibilities

- Be clear about the objectives of the conference and consider what would be best for your province and for Rico Futuro. (What is there to gain and lose?)
- What are your views of what makes a government a good one? Do the Revolutionary Principles meet your needs/desires? Your province's?
- Are you staunch in your beliefs or are you willing to compromise on certain issues?
- Keep a daily journal about the business of each day. What issues were discussed? What positions did you take? Did you speak? Were you swayed by anyone's arguments? Whose and why? If not, why not?
- Be prepared to be an active participant in writing the Revised Revolutionary Principles.

Map 1 of Rico Futuro

Rico Futuro

Map 2 of Rico Futuro

1. Rent-Mo'
2. Hear-Hemp-Win
3. Krow-Ney
4. Chat-Mause
5. Griviani
6. Snaplivea

7. Drilshand
8. Wardale
9. Dylan-arm
10. Regagio
11. Nail-rock
12. Eastern Territory

Province Details

Rent-Mo': Primarily composed of subsistence farmers, this province was somewhat detached from the Revolution. The economy makes some money from banana and coffee exports to North America and Europe. The inhabitants are fiercely independent people, friendly with Hear-Hemp-Win but quite distrustful of Krow-Ney.

Hear-Hemp-Win: An Incan name meaning Land of Mountains and Jungle, this has become a farming province, its people proud of taming a jungle frontier. They also produce lumber from their vast rain forests. They would like to expand their territory into the eastern jungle and hardly use the one outlet they have to the Amazon, satisfied to trade through Rent-Mo'.

Krow-Ney: One of the "Big Three," a powerful, economically self-sufficient province with a large import-export business, Krow-Ney suffered some of the harshest attacks during the Revolution. Many of the Krow-Ney Provincial Councilors believe they could be an independent nation, particularly if they could get Chat-Mause and Griviani to join them. Krow-Ney boasts the nation's capital city of El Dorado, has some industry there, and its eastern side is filled with productive cocoa, coffee, and tobacco farms.

Chat-Mause: Second of the "Big Three" and named by its French and German settlers, Chat-Mause is similar to Krow-Ney in its economic diversity. It has a major commercial port city, St. Boon, which is second only to El Dorado in imports/exports. The eastern half of the province is rich in tobacco, coffee, and cocoa, and many of the revolutionary leaders came from Chat-Mause.

Griviani: The third of the "Big Three," Griviani is composed of large-tract farms (Fazendas) growing coffee and citrus fruits, and employing thousands of Indian/Mestizo laborers—a tradition begun when the Spanish, French, Portuguese and Italians colonized (subjugated) the natives. Glad to be free of their colonial oppressors, Grivianians are very suspicious of outside influences, even from neighboring provinces. They are doing better than most economically.

Snaplivea: Only a step behind "The Big Three," Snaplivea is a liberal province, very active during the Revolution. There is a major city, the provincial capital of Omnipopuli which is the pride of the province. Unlike Griviani, Snaplivea is *not* wary of its neighbors. It is mostly a society of small farms, fishermen, and, in Omnipopuli, merchants. They have not continued the practice of using Indian/Mestizo laborers, and Snapliveans favor a strong, united, and expansive provincial country. They are deeply concerned about the present economic problems of the nation, as well as the potential threats from outside.

"The Little Five"

Drilshand: Land locked and without access to the Amazon, Drilshand is a relatively poor province and its inhabitants see their future in the East, where they hope to expand into the territorial jungle—without interference from neighbors but *with* military support if necessary.

Wardale: Very similar to Drilshand, Wardale is a land of small, somewhat poor farmers. Lacking commerce, Wardale would like to be left alone, for the most part, trading with its neighbors and living in peaceful security. The economic depression is beginning to take its toll, however, and its representatives are eagerly attending the conference, hoping for Revisions that will help them.

Dylan-arm: Named for the German military leader who defeated (originally enslaved) Incas (Hans Zimmer-Dylan, a huge man with huge arms who acquired his nickname from the English mercenaries he used) Dylan-arm is an agricultural region in turmoil. With small farmers, for the most part, and with an Incan/Mestizo work force, Dylan-arm is sinking economically. Fearful of its neighbors, Dylan-arm feels a need for change in the provinces to "Re-Assert" the Revolutionary Principles. "Independence is not enough!" is the motto of this province.

Regagio: Influenced by the Italian/German/Spanish settlers from Argentina, Regagio is a farming and livestock province—the "youngest" and least settled of the provinces, and the least sophisticated politically (they can barely get it together to send a Representative to the Council). This province has a large Indian/Mestizo population, no cities, and a weak economy.

Nail-rock: An eastward-looking province, Nail-rock trades extensively with Brazil, across the Amazon Basin, shipping teak and exotic lumber, cocoa, and coffee (farmed by oppressed Mestizos/Indians) to the Atlantic coast. Far from Krow-Ney, Chat-Mause and Griviani, Nail-rock considers itself the leader and "Guardian" of the Little Five, and some of the leaders of Nail-rock foresee the possible development of a separate country composed of the Little Five, allied with Brazil.

Rico Futuro Census and Indebtedness, 1985

Province	Population	Debt
Rent-Mo'	150,000	($250,000)
Hear-Hemp-Win	140,000	($ 75,000)
Krow-Ney	340,000	($4,500,000)
Chat-Mause	3800,000	($3,500,000)
Griviani	690,000	($5,000,000)
Snaplivea	435,000	($3,000,000)
Drilshand	70,000	($250,000)
Wardale	60,000	($500,000)
Dylan-arm	320,000	($125,000)
Regagio	83,000	($500,000)
Nail-rock	395,000	($2,500,000)

Eastern Territory—approximately 100,000 inhabitants
Total Population: 5,165,000

The Economic Problem

The Unified Provinces of Rico Futuro owe:

$11,700,000 to foreigners (Swiss banks, allies, arms dealers, etc.);

$42,000,000 to private banks and bondholders

The Individual Provinces owe $22,000,000 (figures above in parentheses): this is owed to soldiers, representatives, bond-buyers, banks, etc.

Post-Convention Activity and Analysis

There are several different ways to finish this simulation and debrief the students afterward. It's possible to have delegates review a daily journal (which you may have assigned) and analyze (and self-assess) their effectiveness at the convention. Students could be asked to read about the actual U.S. Constitutional Convention and compare/contrast it to their work (this could be a written or oral presentation). Or, they could be asked to write an editorial for Rico Futuro's leading newspaper, or to create several political cartoons about the convention, or illustrate several dramatic moments, as they saw it.

What is most important in the debriefing of a simulation like this is to focus on the specific skills you want to help students improve. The simulation is designed to provoke critical thinking and problem solving, but it also can be used to improve a variety of literacy skills both during and after the activity. As was mentioned, a text-based Socratic seminar about any of the writings in the Delegate's Packet or those assigned by the teacher could also be accompanied by a written assignment that asks for analysis, synthesis, or evaluation by the student.

What is important to note about the Rico Futuro simulation is that the students are at the center of the activity in the classroom. The simulation will only be as successful as they make it, the responsibility is theirs, and the teacher needs to emphasize that from the beginning. The teacher's responsibility is to make sure that students not only hone their literacy skills, but also learn about the content of the activity; so, the teacher must contextualize the content material for the students, helping them to see the connection between what they did and what the historic parallel was.

Connection to material that will be studied later in the course should also be part of what the teacher must introduce during the debriefing of the simulation. It would also be possible to begin preparing students for standardized test taking by creating a Rico Futuro multiple-choice exam. Once again, the students can be at the center of this activity. If students are assigned, according to their roles, to create three *fair* (not trivial) multiple-choice questions about the events surrounding the simulation, several important things occur. First, the students and teacher must look at how multiple-choice tests are created and designed. This alone will give students insight into how to take a standardized test. Next, students must make decisions about what constitutes information that is important enough to include in a good, fair question, *and* they also have to develop *at least* one believable alternative. Again, this begins to give the students test-taking strategies, increasing the likelihood of their success on future tests. Finally, students will have to discuss and study with their classmates to prepare for all the questions the other delegates create.

The teacher, once again, serves more as a coach during this activity—and can also guide how the questions are phrased, can be the arbiter of "fairness" of questions, and can make the students consciously aware of the fact that they are learning important test-taking strategies through this exercise. Thus, although the Rico Futuro simulation may look like it takes "too much time" to be practical, it is actually a fine example of "less is more," because students will be developing critical-thinking and problem-solving skills, improving their literacy skills, and finishing up by developing test-taking strategies and skills.

Another Approach to "Covering" Content

Before examining some other specific student-centered activities, I'd like to address the content-coverage issue one more time. Again, I'll initially look at an American history example, but, as has been mentioned before, the methodology employed here could be adapted to any other social studies/history course of study. What will be examined here derives from the basic chronological approach to teaching history (U.S. and others). Although there is no research that has ever shown teaching history chronologically is more effective than a thematic or interdisciplinary (or any other) approach, it is still the predominant method used in secondary classrooms. What I suggest is that if a teacher's "comfort zone" for teaching social studies/history is the chronological model, maybe there's another way to approach it.

Let's consider examining parallel periods of American history (giving credence to the notion that "history repeats itself") using an *over/under* time line. For example, what if we were to study the periods from 1865 to 1900 AND 1965 to 2000 this way:

1865	1875	1885	1895	1900
1965	1975	1985	1995	2000

There are some common themes that connect these two eras: race relations, immigration, political scandals, international war, technological growth, and the rise of conservative politics tied to business expansion. Given this format, these 70 years of history could be "covered" (in half the time) by creating a student-centered research and exhibition project.

By dividing the class into teams—six nineteenth-century teams and six twentieth-century teams—with each team assigned one of the themes, *the class*, not the teacher, can fill in the time line. In the process, the students will learn:

- ◆ to do some basic research
- ◆ to create a presentation that other students will have to learn from
- ◆ to develop an assessment to ensure that the class learns what the team has determined are the most important aspects of their theme (critical thinking skills)

♦ to engage in an analytical exercise (writing, discussion, graphic organizers, etc.) comparing and contrasting the two periods.

The teacher's role in all this, of course, is to *front-load* the work. It is the teacher's responsibility to make sure that all of this assignment is clearly organized *before* the students start any work. Therefore, the teacher must be clear about what each team's responsibilities are. The teacher must make sure there are enough research materials available in the classroom and the media center/library. Students will have to know *exactly* what their assignment expectations are *each step of the way* as they proceed through the Time Line Project. So, what materials would students see?

First, there needs to be an assignment sheet that clearly describes not only what the project is, but also clearly states the project's *objectives*. Students need a clear target to aim at. If they are to improve their research skills, the assignment must clearly delineate what kind of information they are gathering, how it will be documented, and in what form it will be submitted for assessment. If oral presentation skills are an objective of the project, students will need to be given clear guidelines or a rubric that *shows* students what the expectations are. If analytical skills are to be improved, students need to know what they are expected to produce to create evidence of that improvement—an essay, a speech, a graphic presentation product, etc. Once again, the class and the project are focused around student activity, responsibility, and learning.

Variations on a Theme

If the 35 years of the over/under time line seem too daunting as an initial project, there are some other overs/unders that might seem more manageable initially. Pairing the 1920s with the 1960s is a fairly natural match and one where students only have to look at a decade's worth of material. However, what a decade each was! By investigating the themes of sports (Babe Ruth, Jack Dempsey, Muhammad Ali, etc.), flight (Lindbergh; the Moonwalk), music (the Jazz Age; the Beatles), drugs (Prohibition; marijuana laws), race (Harlem Renaissance; Civil Rights), and women (suffrage; feminism) students can not only gain a comprehensive sense of the history of each decade, but can engage in serious research into topics and ideas that are still quite vibrant today. In the earlier project, it was suggested that students be divided into teams to conduct their research. An element that should be considered when creating any of these projects is: how much student *choice* can, will, or should be included in the design? This can be a very significant element, particularly regarding student engagement. The 20s/60s over/under project enables the curriculum designer to build in quite a bit of choice for students because of the wide variety of themes, and their subsequent subtopics. Although building certain topics into the design is required, there is, nonetheless, latitude in *how* students present their work, about what kinds of collaboration might be possible (does the Lindbergh researcher present with the Apollo researchers? And do the students have some *choice* in that?), and what variety of assessments might come out of this one project (a written piece, political cartoons, a video clip with analysis, a journal in the "voice" of an historic figure from the time, etc.). Once again, in reviewing this over/under decade project, consider what can be accomplished on two major fronts

1. Twenty years can be "covered" in the time it might have taken to only do ten.
2. Students have to actively engage in doing research, creating a presentation, and teaching each other the significance of, and connections between, the respective decades.

For those who haven't tried presenting U.S. history content material this way, the over/under decade project might be a good place to begin.

Before leaving this area, I'd like to present one more over/under possibility, simply because it is so rich in *content*, yet still provides the elements of a student-centered classroom in which knowledge is *constructed* by actively engaged students. The periods 1828–1860 and 1928–1960 have several dramatic themes in common that would, again, provide students with not only the content that generally gets "covered" in most standard survey courses, but also several very significant *concepts* that have meaning in the world around them today. Consider the themes of federal versus state power (doing case studies of Jackson and Roosevelt, for example, as well as any number of Supreme Court cases), race relations (obviously slavery and emerging civil rights), expansion and international war (Manifest Destiny and the Cold War, not to mention the Mexican War and World War II), and economics (the boom-bust cycles of the American economy through both periods). And, once again, the curriculum designer can determine how students will construct their knowledge of the periods, how they will document their work, how they will present their findings, and how they might create assessments to make sure they know the *most important* content and concepts from the periods in question.

If we were faced with a global studies or world cultures curriculum, we could use the same basic approach in a variety of ways. For example, if students have to learn about regions of the world (Asia, Africa, the Middle East, or Latin America), the teacher needs to consider which countries are most significant to study and then think about what concepts would be most appropriate to engage students in their work. This is also a curriculum that lends itself excellently for analysis by the G.R.E.A.S.E.S. system, adding an additional "G" at the beginning for **G**eography. Beyond the G-G.R.E.A.S.E.S. formula, however, when dealing with world cultures and their histories, there are some basic concepts that the curriculum designer can consider. The development of culture and government; the effects of colonialism, rebellion, revolution, and war; post-colonialism; globalism; and economics are just some of the themes that could be applied to any of the world cultures students would study. In the process, as with the over/ under approach, teachers could "compress" the curriculum (particularly using graphic organizers) so that a class could be divided in a way that a variety of countries or regions could be studied and then compared to each other. Thus, for example, if we had to study Asia, we might divide the class into small groups, or pairs, assigning each a particular country. All groups or pairs would then be asked to investigate geography, government, religion, and economics for their country. Again, providing students with *clear expectations* for their work (how it will be documented, what specifics they definitely need to research, etc), will result in effective learning for all involved.

So, if we were going to investigate "The Ancient World" in China, Japan, Korea, India, Vietnam, and Cambodia, we could ask students to consider the following questions to guide their inquiry:

♦ How did *geography* influence the development of civilization in this culture? What are the major *geographic* features we should be aware of?

♦ What kinds of *government* did the people of this culture develop? Was the *government* closely tied to *religion*?

♦ What were the *religious beliefs* of these peoples at this time?

♦ How did people make a living? What were the *economics* based on? What was valuable, what was necessary to survive?

A final exhibition for a project like this might be that students have to present their findings and provide the class with the information on a simple chart, like the one below.

Themes for Study in Asia's Ancient World

	China	*Japan*	*Korea*	*India*	*Vietnam*	*Cambodia*
Geography						
Government						
Religion						
Economics						

Students would then be responsible for learning the information presented by thier classmates, and, as noted before, creating multiple-choice questions to assess whether their classmates actually learned the information they deemed most important.

Although the questions being asked of the students are ones that are logical and generally asked in even the most traditional classes, the context in which the students have to apply them is what distinguishes their use. It is not just a matter of one or two students raising their hands and answering while others diligently take notes. The purpose of designing curriculum this way is to actively engage *every* student in the work at hand; students have to construct knowledge *from* the questions, not simply answer them. And, as a follow-up activity, asking students to evaluate the cultures, and to synthesize their knowledge through careful compare/contrast analysis, leads students to higher-order thinking, reinforces their content knowledge, and helps them perform better on standardized tests.

Extra! Extra! Read All about It!: The Family Business Project

It is not unusual for social studies/history teachers, in the course of a year, to assign a newspaper project to their students (although this seems to occur in middle schools far more frequently than high schools). Very often, the project covers a brief period of history, familiarizing students with the content of the time and, hopefully, teaching them some nuts and bolts about reading the newspaper (what's an editorial? what's an op-ed?). In keeping with the basic theme of this chapter, I'd like to suggest another way to do a newspaper project—one that involves covering a greater period of history and that again puts the students at the center of the process.

The "Family Business Project" was designed to familiarize students with the important issues in United States history from the federalist era through the election of 1824. Over a three-week period, students, who had been broken into four teams (each representing a "family"), would have to produce three editions of four newspapers. Each family's newspaper represented a specific regional point of view on the issues of the day during the period 1792 through 1824. As you can see by looking at the student assignment sheet, the family descriptors, and the grading rubric, students were given very specific targets to shoot for, and their tasks are very clearly laid out. What does not show up on the assignment sheet, which evolved *after* the project began, was the decision to award "Pulitzer Prizes" for Best Reporting, Best Editing, Best Editorial, Best Column, Best Political Cartoon, and Best Op-Ed piece. Students could not vote for their own newspaper and, after each of the three editions came out, the class voted their awards. This is significant because it brings up yet another form of student assessment and an important form of peer assessment. Once the prizes were voted for and awarded, students discussed why they thought the winners were the deserving parties. In the process, the higher-order thinking skills of analysis and evaluation were quite evident. And, once again, this is a project that puts the responsibility on the students, asking them to work collaboratively, to make critical judgment about content, to understand point of view and perspective, *and* to write with that bias! Students then have to critically evaluate each other's work and explain why and how regionalism in the United States led to so many different points of view. In the process of discussing that conceptual issue (regionalism), students *have to* use specific content materials (the Farewell Address, the Compromise of 1820, etc.) to make their case and explain their point of view—or someone else's. Throughout this process, they have a rather clear sense of their level of achievement because they have already seen the rubric they'll be graded with.

To reinforce what has been said all along: students will learn more and retain what they learn longer if they are actively engaged in constructing meaning around content. The Family Business Project is a prime example of this. Students have to actively engage in understanding a body of content knowledge and then apply a variety of literacy skills to create a product that presents their interpretation of historic events based on a regional point of view. Although developing important higher-order thinking skills, a project like this also embeds the content knowledge more deeply because *the student* has actively engaged in *applying* the knowledge and has not just listened to information being transmitted. Finally, students can be asked to develop multiple-choice questions about the content issues and, in the process, be better prepared to take any standardized test on this, or any other, material.

On the pages that follow you can examine the student assignment sheet, the family descriptors, and the grading rubric for the project.

The Family Business Project
(or, "You, too, can be Citizen Kane!")

♦ You will be given "family" identity, with the characteristics of that family explained to you: that is, where the family is from, what its economic status is (how they made/make their money), what the family members' political philosophy and religious background is, etc. The "family" group you will be affiliated with is that branch of the family that runs *the* prominent newspaper in your region of the country. Each member of your "family" will have a role as an *editor* or *reporter* for the newspaper.

♦ Your Family/Newspaper Staff will receive a list of events that are the stories you have to cover for the paper. Remember, you are the most prominent newspaper in your region and, therefore, strongly represent the views of your part of the country (based on your background as well).

♦ You will conduct staff meetings to determine how you will cover the stories you are presented with: What's your lead story? What will you write editorials about? What will your columnists comment on? Will you have some letters to the editor? You should be able to clearly explain why you have made the choices you have.

♦ You will be given deadlines for producing your newspaper and, on that date, you will receive copies of the other three newspapers from the class and compare/contrast how stories were covered: Similarities? Differences? Why?

Each member of each Family/Newspaper Staff is expected to be totally familiar with every issue covered in that paper. Everyone is expected to be keep a nightly "diary," written from your family member's point of view and due when the project is completed.

News Stories		
First Edition	**Second Edition**	**Third Edition**
The National Bank The Whiskey Rebellion The Farewell Address Proclamation of Neutrality Alien and Sedition Acts Virgina and Kentucky Resolutions The Revolution of 1800	Jeffersonian Democracy Maybury v. Madison The Louisiana Purchase Lewis and Clark Fletcher v. Peck The War of 1812	Tariffs (1816) Florida Dartmouth v. Woodward McCulloch v. Maryland Gibbons v. Ogden Missouri Compromise The Monroe Doctrine The Election of 1824

The Family Business Newspaper Project: Family Descriptors

Adams: You are a New England family, tracing your relatives to the Mayflower. You still have relatives in England. Your family has been staunchly Federalist and fought for the adoption of the Constitution in 1788. Although several members of the family are small farmers, the bulk of the Adams economic interests is in shipping and commerce. The younger family members have expressed an interest in moving to the new Northwest (Ohio) Territory to speculate in real estate and farming. The older family members are discussing investing in new industries in Massachusetts, Rhode Island, and New Hampshire. Your religious background is Puritan, you oppose slavery, and you see yourselves as patrons of the arts.

Smith: A southern family, you trace your roots to the James-town colony. Many members of your family remained neutral during the Revolution because of economic and familial ties to England. Some of your ancestors have been members of the Virginia House of Burgesses. Your political background is Jef-fersonian, and you strongly believe in states' rights. You sup-ported the Articles of Confederation. You own several planta-tions (tobacco, indigo, and, recently, cotton), you own slaves ("They are an economic necessity") and you see your family as "aristocratic" in nature. The younger members of the family are looking to move to the new Southwest territory with inter-ests in small farms, cotton, trapping, and shipping across the trans-Mississippi area. The older family members are en-sconced in politics from Virginia to Georgia. Your religious background is Anglican.

Clark: You live in the Northwest Territory, originally moving from the New York, New Jersey, Pennsylvania region. Your background is Dutch-German and your ancestors fought in the Revolution for America! You believe in a strong central government but are *not* a Federalist in principle. You have be-gun farming and trapping in the Northwest and are often be-set with Indian "problems." You are against slavery, and the younger members of the family are looking across the Missis-sippi for new farmland and river-shipping business. You feel somewhat threatened on the frontier, yet, at the same time, you are, by nature, aggressive frontierspeople at heart.

Jackson: Born on the western Virginia border, the patriarch of your clan moved to the Tennessee/Kentucky region after fighting in the Revolution. Small farmers and land speculators comprise most of the family. Younger members of the family find New Orleans, the Mississippi, and the Texas frontiers particularly attractive. Priding yourselves as Indian fighters, you also see slavery as "necessary," and, if possible, a comfort-able luxury. You won't interfere with someone else's right to own a slave. You are a rugged, aggressive, individualistic frontier family. Government, to you, should be a local "ser-vant." How can anyone so far away, in Washington, D.C., serve your needs?

Family Business Assessment Criteria

A
- Wrote grammatically correct, correctly spelled articles that clearly represent the regional point of view of your family in a persuasive manner.
- Researched the historic events of each period with thoroughness, as evidenced in your written article and class discussions.
- Used your time, in class and outside of class, effectively (as witnessed by the teachers and as reflected in your work).
- Worked cooperatively and responsibly in your group, meeting deadlines, helping others by offering constructive suggestions, and exerting leadership or team spirit throughout.
- You were able to clearly explain and defend your articles in class discussions and debates, responding appropriately to questions and challenges.

B
- Wrote a persuasive article identifiable as representing your region's point of view, with few grammatical and spelling errors.
- Researched the historic events with detail but not complete thoroughness, missing some of the subtlety of the issues.
- Basically, you used your time effectively, seldom being asked to get back on task or seldom failing to have work ready when you arrived at class.
- Worked well with your family teammates, meeting most deadlines and accepting your role with energy.
- You were able to explain and defend your article, clarifying misunderstandings or disputed prints, if not always convincing opponents of your stance or accuracy.

C
- Wrote an article that presented the facts about an historic event, but didn't thoroughly or clearly identify the regional point of view related to it.
- Researched historic events, recording basic facts without probing for depth or insight.
- Generally, you used your time effectively, but too often had to be "reminded" to get back to task; work brought to class was satisfactory but not distinguished in its quantity or quality.
- Worked with your teammates to meet the paper's deadlines, but you would not impress anyone with your "team spirit" or leadership within the group. At times, you seemed to be working only for yourself.
- You were able to explain the core facts of your article(s) without totally, or clearly, convincing questioners or challengers of your accuracy or position.

D
- Wrote an article, but seriously confused facts or misrepresented issues.
- Only minimally researched your topics.
- Misused class time and resources more than half of the time.
- Barely worked with your teammates; missed deadlines; grudgingly complied with team goals.
- You were only minimally able to explain the facts of your story, without elaboration or accuracy.

F
- You did not get your articles completed.
- You failed to do any effective research.
- You abused class time designated for work and failed to do related homework.
- You did not work with teammates; you proved to be detriment to your group because of your lack of work or poor work attitude.
- You were not able to explain your topic in discussion or debate.

5

Where Do We Go from Here?: Implementing the Student-Centered Secondary Classroom

First and foremost, implementing student-centered classrooms will involve change, something schools do not "do" particularly well. This kind of change can occur at a number of different levels, and it is important to examine each constituency that can help create student-centered classrooms. Simply put, implementing this kind of change can happen:

♦ at the individual classroom level, initiated by a teacher;

♦ on a team level, initiated by a group of teachers;

♦ on a building level, initiated by an administration with teacher and parent support;

- on a district level, initiated and supported by the
  school board *and* the teacher union; and
- on a state level, through the development of in-
  centives by legislative and policy agents.

By examining each of these constituencies closely, we can
see how each could effectively contribute to the move toward
student-centered classrooms. Before we do that, it needs to be
said, once again, that change is a difficult process. In *The Performance Assessment Handbook* (Vol. One), I included a list of 38
items that were under the heading "There's always a (good?)
reason not to change." It need not be repeated here, as I'm sure
any group of educators could quickly assemble a similar list,
just as I'm sure many of the items on that list would be among
those brainstormed by said group. The point is a simple one,
however, and it is that unless people have the *will* to change
and are willing to make a commitment to changing what they
do, things will stay the same. The most significant aspect
about this call to change is that it is focused on the students
and, therefore, any objection or obstruction can only be seen as
self-serving or purely selfish. Why wouldn't educators want
to implement a program that makes their students more engaged learners and more effective students?

The intent here is to neither sound glib nor self-righteous.
Change is difficult. It takes time. It is a slow process. But, you
need not do it all at once, *and* you need not do it alone. Incremental implementation (as described in Chapter 2) by a committed group of teachers has a far better chance at succeeding
than a crash course that tries to change everything at once
(which often leads to a conservative reaction that reverts
things to the way they were before the change was attempted).
This kind of change needs support from a variety of sources. It
needs parental support. It needs genuine, committed, high-
quality and ongoing staff development. All those constituencies mentioned earlier need to take an active role in supporting this kind of change and that is what we need to consider
now, to see how each can contribute to the implementation of
a student-centered secondary classroom.

What Can the Teacher Do?

Interestingly, I have spent 30 years in schools and never met a member of the "curriculum police." For all the talk of standards and testing and so on, teachers still have a remarkable amount of autonomy *in their classroom*. Yes, there certainly is greater attention paid to certain test scores, and there are teachers who are fearful that if their students don't perform well on those tests, the teacher's job will be in jeopardy. Realistically, only in the most draconian systems does this happen—and, even then, the teacher (if s/he is tenured) gets transferred, not fired. Nonetheless, it is a fear that is out there and needs to be addressed. What I contend is that if teachers engage their students in more active learning, the test scores improve and the students actually retain more of what they learned. There have been scores of shows such as *60 Minutes* and *Oprah* that have publicized active, engaged "youth" who are achieving "against all odds." This results from dedicated teachers, of course, and from teachers who have recognized that students need to learn how to construct knowledge, not regurgitate it.

So, what can you, as an individual teacher, do, assuming you want to get with the program? Here are some simple steps I'd recommend:

- Take a look at your curriculum and decide where there are "natural" topics, themes, or units with which to do student-centered work.
- Plan, plan, plan.
- Try a small unit with your best class first. Remember, the first time you do something, it's seldom very successful (First time you rode a bike? Drove a clutch car? Taught a class?). Give yourself a chance to be somewhat successful and to learn how to do this well.
- Make sure you and the students are clear about the objectives of what you are doing. If you can develop a rubric (preferably *with* your students), that would be helpful in setting some clear targets.

- Get feedback from the students—find out what they thought was good or bad, what was hard or easy, and what they learned from or not.

- Develop a "Plan B" for your "plan, plan, plan."

- Don't think you've hit a roadblock when it's only a speed bump. Slow down and take a look around. What needs to be changed or tweaked?

- Find colleagues, administrators, and parents to share the ideas with, and with whom you can engage in meaningful dialogue about how to make this most effective (I know about the "time" problems most teachers have, but that is addressed later).

What Can the Team Do?

Teams can implement student-centered classrooms in a number of ways, including the use of interdisciplinary, multidisciplinary, and integrated curriculum. Too often, interdisciplinary curriculum is confused with *coordinated* curriculum. For example, while the English/language arts teacher is working on *Huckleberry Finn*, the social studies/history teacher focuses on the geography of the Mississippi River. Although this is a *coordinated* effort, it is not interdisciplinary teaching. An interdisciplinary unit would be driven by a question or theme that would be used in *both* classes and allow for deeper study of the subject matter. Thus, students would read *Huckleberry Finn* in *both* English/language arts and social studies/history, focusing on a question like, "How are race relations portrayed in the novel *Huckleberry Finn*?" The teachers could then introduce students to the particular lenses of their respective disciplines as they examine the novel, bringing in sources to enhance the study. Critical reviews from Twain's time, as well as contemporary ones, could be used to see how the work has been viewed over time. Students could be broken into *critical study teams* to examine particular sections of the book and then present their findings. They could be asked how the basic themes of the book could be translated into a contemporary television series or a movie. Student-centered activities involving higher-order critical thinking could be expressed with a variety of products—illustrations (imagine Jim and Huck as gang members!), videotaped productions, critical reviews and op-ed pieces, debates, role-plays, and a host of others could be implemented. So, rather than just examining the text in a rather formal and traditional fashion, while exploring the geography of the Mississippi, students would be asked to engage in a deep and serious critical examination of the text the same way historians, social scientists, and literary critics do!

Teams can also implement *multidisciplinary units* for their students. Again, this is *not* the unit where the social studies/history class is studying the Civil War, so the English/language arts reads *The Red Badge of Courage*, the science teacher is asked to investigate anesthesia and amputation, and the poor math teacher is told, "Oh, do something about statistics of body counts and whatever." Multidisciplinary study must emanate from a common objective *among* the subject disciplines (this means teachers, of course, must have *time* to plan together). A genuine *multidisciplinary unit* would be created by way of teachers talking together and deciding that students need to learn about several basic, important concepts like statistics, economics, empathy, and analysis. Based on *those* outcomes, teachers could then decide how to teach this historical period. So, in fact, the math teacher might look at the proportional relationship of Northern soldiers to Southern soldiers killed in the war in the context of reading *The Red Badge of Courage* and considering what it means to have a "civil war" in a country. Again, the particular lenses of the specific disciplines would be aimed at engaging the students in *constructing* knowledge based on the subject matter being studied. And, please note, science was left out of this multidisciplinary unit.

If we were to look at a truly *integrated* unit, our focus might change entirely. We might remove ourselves from the traditional curriculum and present our students with problems like the ones that follow (these were developed for students who were entering the "first wave" of charter schools in Massachusetts in 1996).

Sample Exhibition Problems
for Integrated Curriculum

Problem 1.
High-Tech Center with Community Center

A foreign conglomerate wants to open a high-technology center along Route 495. They want to include a community center in their plans, as a goodwill/public relations gesture. They have approached your consulting firm with their proposition and asked you to consider the following aspects of the project:

+ What would be the best technologies (personal computers, defense tech, telecommunications, etc.) to focus on and why? [Students would have to do market analysis breakdowns, historical inquiry of the area, research on the conglomerate, etc.]

+ Where would the best site location be and why? [This would require real-estate analysis, a critical look at demographics, as well as predictive studies/surveys]

+ What should the community center focus on? [Students would have to conduct surveys and interviews, as well as conduct resource searches regarding the center as a venue for a variety of arts. They would also have to see what the community needs for sports or an athletic center. Is this a possible venue for trade fairs, etc.]

+ What should the physical plant look like? What physical design(s) would be aesthetically pleasing yet cost effective?

You will be expected to present your findings to a panel of experts from the conglomerate for their consideration. You should have clear documentation of findings available, including final reports, process journals, records of work done, sources of information, cost breakdowns, etc.

Problem 2. Charter School

You have been approached by members of your community who want to start a charter school. They invite you to be on their Founders Committee and, liking the idea, you accept. They have asked you, as a committee member, to respond to several concepts and to investigate several others. You will present your ideas and findings to them when the committee meets to consolidate its reports into an application to the state. Here's the list of items the committee has presented to you:

♦ What should the major goals of the school be—and why?

♦ How large (number of students) should the school be, and what should the student body "look like" (diversity)—and why?

♦ Given your ideas about the number of students, design a physical plant for the school (be creative).

♦ What must students do to earn a diploma—and why? (Should there be required courses? Should there be traditional departments, tests, etc.?)

♦ What is the best financing plan the school can devise?

♦ Describe the teachers you would like to hire—how might they differ from "traditional" teachers; how might the "job description" regarding the teachers' roles and responsibilities at your school differ from such a description at a "traditional" school?

♦ What controversies do you anticipate—and what are your counterarguments?

Problem 3.
Solar-Powered Public Transportation

Ford, GM, and Chrysler have combined their energies to offer a huge ($) prize if someone will present them with a prototype for a solar-powered public transportation system. Your engineering team has been approached to enter this contest. Here are the guidelines for winning.

- ◆ The basic vehicle for transportation must be designed to use solar power, but must also have a "back-up" emergency system that is a cheap and ecologically-responsible power source.
- ◆ Which cities in the world would be the prime candidates for using this system?
- ◆ How and where (in what ways) can computer technologies be applied to maximize the design and use of the new system?
- ◆ What public transportation systems (worldwide and historically) have proven most efficient and successful and why? How can we apply their success to our design/proposal?

Problem 4.
The In-Between Museum

Parents from five suburban Boston communities have been particularly impressed by Boston's Childrens' Museum and the hands-on Museum of Science. Their interest is in creating what they are calling "The In-Between Museum," "a place for teenagers." They have several distinct requirements:

- ◆ they want it to address popular culture (particularly music and the arts), sports, science, and world issues;
- ◆ they want a physical design that will require that someone entering the museum will have to pass through each of the focus areas before they can exit;
- ◆ they want it to be hands-on and engaging.

The Parents Committee has a site and the financial backing of several foundations. They have asked you to design their museum for them.

These problems are all truly integrated, requiring students to *use* all the core disciplines to reach their solutions. They also, very clearly, take *time* to do. Students would have to work in teams, do a vast amount of research, do fieldwork, and then compile data in a way to devise solutions to the problems presented. They would *not* have to regimentally march from English to math to social studies to science to attack these problems. Quite the reverse would be in effect. They would first have to examine the challenge presented (just like adults in the "real" world) *and then* decide what they need to know in each of the academic disciplines. The learning would have true *meaning* to the students because the problems are just as authentic as those that adults face each day in the "real" world.

Teams of teachers, created by choice, not fiat, can develop curriculum like this. *They* can decide whether to coordinate, or do interdisciplinary, multidisciplinary, or integrated curriculum. Whatever the case, their choice needs to be made based on what's best for their students. One other matter needs to be stated about teams: there need to be rules that teams operate around; otherwise, they will not succeed. These rules are:

- ♦ Teams can't be created by administrative fiat ("Just because we have the same uniform on doesn't mean we're a team!"). Staff development is necessary. *And,* teaming shouldn't only be seen as a middle-school concept. High schools could also benefit greatly from *effective* teaming.

- ♦ Teams need to work effectively *and* efficiently together. This means:
  - ○ Meetings need an agenda (that is followed!).
  - ○ Meetings need a "Designated Facilitator" (to short-circuit digressions, to stay focused on the agenda, and to prevent meetings from becoming child-study sessions or gripe sessions).

- ♦ Teams need to set clear goals for students and themselves, and to periodically assess their progress.

If teachers, parents, administrators, and district personnel could truly engage in productive dialogue about the value of *teaming* teachers, much of the above could happen. But teachers must promote the idea first. Historically, teaching has been an isolated and insulated profession where everyone has been, essentially, an independent contractor. Although this may be consoling to some, it misses the point. All professions benefit from practitioners working collaboratively, sharing ideas, methods, strategies, and technologies. Teaching, as a profession, has lagged behind far too long in this respect. It is time to move into the twenty-first century with energy and purpose. It is time to move out of our insulted, isolated classrooms and become citizens of our school community; it is time to invite parents and administrators in to see the good work we do. Teaming is a wonderful step in that direction. We can learn from each other, and we can do better work *because* of each other. It's time to move in new directions.

What Can Happen on the School/Building Level?

As noted in the first bullet on the preceding page, administrators cannot legislate teaming, or student-centered teaching, or any other innovation by fiat. In the twenty-first century, administrators have to recognize that their role needs to be that of a *facilitator*, not just a manager. Administrators will need to facilitate opportunities for teachers to work together, to observe one another's teaching, to attend conferences and workshops that improve their expertise, and so on. Administrators, in dialogue with teachers and parents, need to be able to propose initiatives that are optimally educational for the students of the school. To do this, they may have to consider looking at school differently than they do now—from the scheduling, to the use of personnel, to communication with the community.

What kinds of things might administrators do that could promote student-centered work occurring in more and more classrooms? Encouraging teachers to take staff development seriously and bringing in people, or using "homegrown" people, who are not theoreticians but practitioners, is one step. An equally important step is to make staff development ongoing and dispense with the one-day, one-shot dog and pony show from supposed "experts." For the most part, teachers have a terribly cynical attitude about staff development, and this attitude has developed because they have to sit through countless hours of what, to them, is fairly useless stuff. Because of that, administrators will have to work all the harder to make staff development an integral part of the culture of the school. Teachers and administrators *must* honestly see themselves as lifelong learners who are curious about finding new and better ways to help their students.

Administrators need to consider their school and its culture organizationally, if they want to encourage more student-centered learning in the classrooms. By "organizationally," I mean the schedule, the class size, and the use of personnel. It is pretty clear, at this point in time, that smaller schools tend to be more effective because students are known by the adults in the school community (we certainly don't see any huge, independent college-preparatory schools with 25 and 30 students in each class, do we?). And, although arguments about class size can present evidence on both sides for why it does or doesn't make a difference (achievement-wise), we certainly know that it makes a difference regarding student attitudes toward their school and their willingness to work hard, stay in school, etc. Administrators need to look at how teacher-to-student ratios can be maximized, as well as how time each day can best be used to provide maximal learning. Too many schools have rather faddishly adopted block scheduling in the past few years. Very often this has been done without conversation, dialogue, or consultation with teachers. Rationales, at the very least, should be provided for why a school is moving to a block schedule. Certainly, it is definitely a model that almost *insists* upon student-centered classroom activity (you can't really lecture for 90 to 100 minutes every day, or even every other day, can you?). To bring in a significant schedule change without first providing open dialogue with teachers and parents, and without creating an ongoing staff development component to support it, is to invite disaster. And, all too often, as was mentioned earlier in this book, these new changes are often given a "pilot year" tryout, with a promise to revert to the traditional schedule if things don't seem to work the first year. Again, this is a recipe for failure. Here is where administrators need to genuinely exert some leadership in helping create consensus among staff, parents, and even students about what changes are needed and why. That's a role administrators can play, which, in the long term, will help promote best practices in the classroom and give *everyone* a chance to succeed.

As far as use of personnel is concerned, administrators need to consider whether it makes sense to have a fair number of professional teachers (who have simply changed their title to things like "guidance counselor," "dean of students," "assistant principal," and so on) *not* working in classrooms with students—and other teachers—as much as possible. This would mean changing our concept of school from the industrial-management, hierarchical model and moving toward a more professional-collaborative scheme (like the models used by doctors, lawyers, and architects). It might mean asking people to rewrite and reconsider their job descriptions. It certainly would require cooperation and support from the teachers' union at most schools and in most districts. Nonetheless, think about how some new deployment of personnel might support some of the other ideas suggested here and, most significantly, support the implementation of more student-centered learning. For example, if guidance or administrative personnel were regular players in the school's classrooms, it wouldn't be difficult for an administrator or counselor to "cover" a teacher's class while that teacher participates in some meaningful staff development for a day or two. Doesn't it make more sense for guidance counselors to observe their students *in the classroom* rather than just knowing a student on paper and having one or two meetings a year? This may mean we will ask teachers to play a more active role as *advisors* and actually change "homeroom" from a logistical, record-keeping time of day to a more meaningful period where school issues and concerns are talked about, where advisors check in with students about their academic progress, etc. It could mean that teachers remain advisors to the same students over three or four (or more) years, really getting to know each student and his/her family. And, it may mean that the teacher will gain valuable insights about the student, over time, that can be shared with colleagues, and make the teaching and learning in the school more effective.

Thus, there is a great deal administrators can do to help a school become more student-centered and for classrooms to become more active and effective settings. While promoting that, the administrator is also the person who must mediate how the community perceives what is happening, and the administrator needs to, of course, deal with the political aspects of testing and standards and the like. This is no easy task. But, administrators do not have an easy job as things stand now, and many seem frustrated that their schools are not the kind of vibrant and energetic places they might be, where students and teachers are engaged in active and exciting learning. There are ways to move in that direction, but collaboration between administrators, teachers, parents, the district administration, and the school board needs to occur in an active, open, and productive fashion, keeping the goals of effective teaching and active learning in the center of the dialogue at all times.

What Can the School District Do?

There are very few multimillion dollar enterprises that open their board of director positions to the public. Yet schools, the last (and only?) bastion of direct democracy, do so on a regular basis. Seldom are the members of district school boards educators themselves. Aside from having attended school, their expertise in the field of education is often fairly limited (this is akin to saying, "I've been driving a car for 25 years so that qualifies me to be on GM's Board of Directors"). Of course, school board members are often people who volunteer their time and have a strong sense of working for their community, and there is no doubt that most of their hearts are in the right place—they want to deliver the best educational "product" to their district. In what ways, then, could the school board and the district administrators help promote more student-centered learning in their classrooms?

For one thing, as was recommended in the last section about building administrators, they could engage in active dialogue with teachers about what would bring about more effective practice in the district. Too often, boards of education and superintendents only deal with union officials, and their business revolves around "labor issues" and cost-efficiency discussions. In all the years I've worked in schools, I've almost never seen school board members or district administrators spend an entire in-service day participating in staff development.

A problem that often prevents innovations from being implemented in classrooms is embedded in a mindset that the only important time a teacher spends in school is when s/he is in *direct contact* with students. The idea of collegial sharing, of teachers having time to reflect on their work and discuss it with each other, is seldom seen as important to the life of the school. In much the same way as building administrators have "faculty meetings," which are really "principal's meetings" (Who makes the agenda? Where does input for the agenda come from? How often could the content of the meeting have been put on a memo and distributed, rather than using a valuable hour or more when you have teachers *together* to talk about teaching and learning?), school boards determine policy about what will go on in the district with little input from the people who will have to implement those policies. How much emphasis (and, thereby, pressure) will the school board and district administrators put on testing—and why? Will any careful analysis go into which are the best tests to use, and will there be careful analysis about the results beyond just looking at "scores?" These are important questions that have a direct impact upon the way schools operate and how teachers perceive their work, and these issues need to be discussed openly and publicly with *all* the constituents at the table.

What's the school board's and district administration's view of staff development? Is it seen as an investment in the improvement of the faculty or as a "day off" that simply fulfills a contract clause? Again, this is a serious issue that should be discussed at every level of the district. Does the board elicit input from the community in a proactive fashion, getting out into the community and talking and listening to parents and students and teachers, or does it simply announce its monthly meeting and "invite" interested parties to attend? This can make a huge difference in the creation of policy, and it can have a significant impact on what goes on in the classrooms of a district.

Do the board and the union leadership try to work collaboratively, or does the history of adversarial strife prevent that? Who needs to take the initiative to help change that dynamic? Certainly, the union must be an advocate for its teachers, but it should also see itself as an advocate for the parents and students of the district, creating a common point of reference with the school board. If district issues focus first on "How does this best benefit teaching and learning in our district?" we might see far more innovation and change, with higher levels of student-centered classrooms being implemented. Of course, there are serious financial issues the board and district administration are responsible for, and I'm not trying to soft-pedal that here, but maybe even those issues would be more easily or amenably resolved if there was a sense of working together to improve the district.

It is not easy being a school board member or a district administrator. There are many constituencies that have to be addressed. There is a state board of education setting policy that needs to be complied with, there are the voters of the district who want the most bang for their buck, there are building administrators who need more of everything, there is a teachers union and a teaching staff that have their own unique perspective on how things should be run, and there are students and parents who want the best from their schools. Working with all these groups is complex, to say the least. But, having some clear goals, particularly around developing an active, engaged, student-centered education, and establishing who will be responsible for the kind of accountability system that needs to be in place, and the kind of dialogue that needs to *consistently* occur around this issue, would be an important first step any school board and district administrators might make. Supporting meaningful and ongoing staff development, along with collaborative teacher time that values cooperative planning and reflection, would be another important step a school board and district administrators could take in moving their schools toward more student-centered learning. Most significantly, weighing the input from all these constituencies and keeping everyone focused on the teaching and learning that needs to be the driving force for the district, the board and district administrators could have a significant impact on the steady improvement and achievement of their schools.

What Can the State/Legislature Do?

Although state education departments and state legislatures have been in the forefront of a number of initiatives in the past few years, those initiatives have primarily focused on testing and "accountability." We are currently experiencing an unprecedented testing mania in this country, primarily spurred on by state education departments and state representatives (it would be refreshing, just once, to see if the legislators who pass the testing laws would submit to taking the tests themselves first, and having *their* scores published in the local newspapers!), and encouraged, certainly, by the federal government. Although this type of "standards and testing from above" does have some effect on schools, it does little to promote serious reform where it is needed—for the individual achievement of each student. As a recent article from the state of Washington commented, "Let no child go untested," is more the aphorism on the state and federal level than the clichéd "Leave no child behind" that the media feeds us with.

Cynicism aside, however, there are certainly positive actions the state could take to move schools toward more student-centered education. And, state legislatures could also take the lead in this area if they would focus on something other than test scores. If both state education departments and state legislative branches demanded to see more genuine evidence of student learning, beyond test scores, it could encourage teachers to create more student-centered classrooms that produced more authentic assessments. The state could also examine how it allocates funds for education (or even allocate more!) and put more money into serious, ongoing staff development, so that teachers could learn more about how to design curriculum, instruction, and assessment that is more student-centered and student-active. The state could take the initiative in promoting peer mentoring and could create leadership institutes for administrators, school boards, teachers, parents, and students. Too often, educators, and those who think about education, are purely *reactive*. We wait until there is a discernible problem and then try to figure out how to solve it. What this entire book is about, really, is about being *proactive*. It is time for educators, and all those who seriously care about and are concerned about education, to *take the initiative*. This means far more than legislating testing every year in "core subjects." That's an easy out that will get predictable results (the suburbs will score high, the cities will score low; the white kids will be winners, the kids-of-color will be losers; rural white kids will also lose—it's as much economic as it is race, of course). No, testing is not the way to genuinely make schools accountable. Taking education seriously enough to look at *how* kids are learning, in classrooms, in schools, and in districts, is the more challenging gauntlet to throw down to our state education departments and our state legislatures.

The state of Rhode Island (under the leadership of Commissioner of Education Peter McWalters) has instituted a multiyear school review process (SALT committees—School Accountability for Learning and Teaching) that sends teachers and administrators out into schools (after undergoing a rigorous preparation process) to provide districts with feedback on what's working and what's not in those schools. It's not an *evaluation* of the schools (although the local newspapers, with their typical myopia, translate it that way) so much as it's a *critique,* the aim of which is improvement. And, significantly, it is a very effective form of professional development for those who serve on the visiting committees. Initiatives like these, as opposed to simply requiring testing (which Rhode Island has *not* done, by the way) focus the public and the educators on the *process* of education, not the simplistic one-day *product* that tests are. Here, again, it would be important for more serious public dialogue and debate to occur to consider how the state education department and the state legislature—no matter what state you are in—could more effectively *improve* the quality of education in the state.

What Can Parents and the Community Do?

Too often, a potentially great resource is lost in the school equation: parents and the community. I mean this in more than the PTA, PTO, or Boosters Club dimension. Because of the way school culture has developed in this country, parents are too often seen as intrusive or troublemakers (because they defend their kids!). It's time to recognize that parents and members of the community are a tremendous resource, potentially, for schools in an array of ways. In terms of sheer person-power, skills, talents, and energy, parents and community members can expand the possibilities of schooling, can support teachers and administrators, and can bring countless elements to bear on improving the school. Educators need to be more amenable to reaching out to parents and the community in positive ways, to inviting them in, and to asking for their counsel, so as to make the education of our students more effective. Parents, do, after all, trust us with their children. We, in turn, should trust them as partners and not treat them as adversaries.

In the same way, parents and community members have to begin to become more active in learning about what's going on in their schools, not in a way that would dictate policy or "boss" teachers and administrators around, but as supportive partners in the educational career of their children. Parents and community members can encourage more student-active, student-centered education in their schools by asking to see the products of student learning, not just report cards and grades. We most often see numbers of parents at school when students are involved in sporting events or dramatic or musical productions. When students perform, parents turn out and *see* what their students can do. In the same way, teachers and parents should want to present what students can do in the *academic* areas, through public exhibitions and performances. If parents would ask for it, teachers would begin to consider it, administrators could support it, and we would begin to see schools where students regularly presented their work in public forums.

Teachers and parents, as well as teachers and community members, need to begin to have more frequent and constructive dialogue about issues like course objectives and content. The once-a-year "open house" is a pro forma cosmetic event that does little to further teachers' or parents' knowledge of each other, thereby decreasing the ability of either one to help their students improve. Teachers need to know more about the worlds their students come from, and parents need to know more about the culture of the school their child attends. This can only happen through regular, positive dialogue between the concerned parties.

Time, of course, is the issue, as it always is in any matter pertaining to school. And it is one that could consume an entire volume. Let it only be said that, if schools begin to restructure in new ways (schedules, teaming arrangements, planning time for teachers, deployment of personnel, etc.) the time needed to accomplish goals—like parents and teachers and community members meeting on a more regular basis—could be found. The constituents need to express the desire to meet first, though, and must see each other as allies aimed at a common goal. If that can happen, schools might begin to look more like what we would like to see them be.

How Will It All Happen?

As mentioned at the beginning of this chapter, change is a difficult process and one that schools do not throw themselves into with reckless abandon. In fact, most schools, at best, adapt to change. James Herndon, in his wonderful book, *How to Survive in Your Native Land* (Boynton/Cook Publishers, 1997), has what I think is an accurate take on schools and change. The following excerpt was originally written in 1971:

> So it is that institutions don't change, but people do. There is no law anymore that people must go to church or pay attention to the church, and so many people don't, while others do. That is the best you can expect, and good enough. You can apparently

get one institution to combat another, and it would be most useful to get rid of the law that all kids have to go to some school or other until age x or any other age. The public school is the closest thing we have to a national established church, Getting-an-Education the closest thing to God, and it should be possible to treat it and deal with it as the church has been treated and dealt with. This treatment has not really changed the existence of the one institution and will not harm the other, but it has allowed the growth of alternatives to it and that is what is wanted, even if some of those alternatives have become, and will become, institutions themselves. (p. 112)

We might do well to heed Herndon and to realize that, ultimately, people can make the difference. Teachers, parents, administrators, school board members, state education department personnel, and state and federal legislators and policy makers could make a difference in how "school happens" in this country.

My extension of Herndon's metaphor, that the public school is the closest thing to an established national church in this country, is to invite people to join a modern Protestant Reformation and begin to consider the alternatives he alludes to. We have seen some of this already, with the charter school movement and the expansion of home schooling, as well as the lively (and sometimes vitriolic) debate over vouchers. But we need to do it in a more consistent and systematic way. We need to encourage public debate and engage all the citizens in our communities to join the discussion. Our students are too important and deserve no less. Our schools can provide opportunity for future generations that recent ones have missed. We *do* need to ask "why do we do what we do the way we do it?" and honestly look at the answers we come up with. Schools that encourage active, energetic learning, where the students are at the center of all the planning, all the decisions, and all the work, is a far nobler goal than "higher test scores"—and a far more important one.

So, taking Herndon's advice, I'll rely on people—on the teachers, the administrators, the parents, the community members, the school board officials, the state education department personnel, and the legislators and policy makers—to make decisions to implement change that will be aimed at improving the *process* of education in this country. If we can begin to get those *people* to talk to each other about issues like the ones raised in this book, I believe we can begin to bring about genuine change in our schools. So, start talking to each other. We have nothing to lose and everything to gain.